LEADER'S GUIDE

Discover your Church
and why you need each other

Rachel Boehm Van Harmelen

CRC Publications
Grand Rapids, Michigan

CRC Publications thanks Rachel Boehm Van Harmelen for writing this course. She is a freelance writer and editor who lives in Ottawa, Ontario.

Unless otherwise indicated, Scripture quotations in this publication are from the HOLY BIBLE, NEW INTERNATIONAL VERSION, © 1973, 1978, 1984, International Bible Society. Used by permission of Zondervan Bible Publishers.

Discover Your Church and Why You Need Each Other. Church school material for early teens, © 2000, CRC Publications, 2850 Kalamazoo Ave. SE, Grand Rapids, MI 49560. All rights reserved. Printed in the United States of America on recycled paper. ⊕

We welcome your comments. Call 1-800-333-8300 or e-mail us at editors@crcpublications.org.

ISBN 1-56212-411-0

10 9 8 7 6 5 4 3 2 1

Contents

How to Use This Course

Getting to know—and actively participate in—their faith community is an important way for early teens to nurture their faith. Together with God's people, teens can gain a powerful sense of belonging, of being cared for and of caring, of being a vital part of a worshiping and ministering congregation.

Discover Your Church and Why You Need Each Other is a six-session course for students in grades 7-8 that offers a lively, "hands-on" exploration of what the church is and how it works. Teens "discover their church" through a variety of activities, including exploring God's Word, interacting with church members, planning a worship service, observing their church in action, using their gifts in the church, and more.

Goals of This Course

- To understand and appreciate our local congregation: its purpose, worship, care, outreach, leadership, and nurture.
- To view our local congregation as a caring family, a place where we are accepted, where we can grow in our faith.
- To use our gifts for the benefit of our congregation and community.

Audience and Settings

Discover Your Church and Why You Need Each Other is aimed at young teens in grades 7-8. For students familiar with the church, the course offers a fresh look that will challenge them to greater understanding and active participation. For students just coming into the church, the course offers an introduction to what it is and how it works. The course is intended to help all students realize that the church cares for them and has a lot of offer them—just as they have a lot to offer to the church.

Discover Your Church was written with the church school class in mind. However, it could also be adapted to retreat settings (adult "guests" could really get to know the kids in an "away from home" location). If your church has a midweek "family night" or education night, think about

offering *Discover Your Church* there, perhaps adapting it to an intergenerational approach—families learning together about the church. Youth groups that are preparing a "youth worship service" could also benefit from the course, focusing mainly on session 2 but drawing in selected activities from the other sessions as well.

Approach

While not sacrificing content and faith knowledge, this course focuses on faith nurture through coming to know and appreciate the local congregation. As much as possible, students will be learning by doing, observing, questioning, thinking, and gathering information, as opposed to being told what the church is like and how it functions. This is in line with good teaching methods and with the findings of an extensive survey by the Protestant Church-Owned Publishers Association (PCPA):

> Young people are used to "doing." They expect interaction. Fun is necessary. At the same time they are willing to think and they have a very introspective side. Many take "spiritual things" seriously and want to know the practical reality of faith. Truth and honesty are essential. They see through a fake and are not interested in easy answers. Engage them in reality and make them respond to it.

One important way to "engage students in reality" is to have them interact with a variety of folks from your congregation. Though inviting various guests is usually optional, doing so will clearly tell your teens that this congregation is actually interested in them and cares about them! For details, please see the section "Scheduling Guests" (p. 6).

Another way to make this course "real" for students is to do one or more of the special events described on page 6 (see "Scheduling Special Events").

Materials

The **student book** helps guide the "discovery" process with Bible studies, creative small group activities, and opportunity for personal response and action. This leader's guide tells you when the student book will be used in the sessions. Order one book for each person in your group, including yourself. Keep the student books in the classroom between sessions. After the course is over, encourage students to keep the book and to refer to it from time to time as a reminder of what they've discovered about the church.

This **leader's guide** gives you detailed plans for six sessions and a basic plan for an extra, seventh session. You'll probably want to glance through all six sessions (or read the summaries below) to gain a sense of where the course is headed. Each session includes

- a focus statement that summarizes the main point or theme of the session.
- a list of the Scripture references used in the session.
- a list of goals that you and the group should achieve in the session.
- an overview of the entire session.
- a list of materials you'll need to lead the session, as well as a list of special guests you may want to invite.
- a session background that gives you insights into the content of the session.
- step-by-step suggestions for reaching the session goals, many including optional approaches.
- a brief section that alerts you to special materials (or guests) needed for the next session.
- session extensions that suggest additional activities, projects, and so on.

Scheduling Special Events

This course can be greatly enhanced by scheduling one or more special events. The course can be taught without these, and you may not be able to do all three. The first of the three listed below is part of the suggested procedure for session 5; if you can do only one of the three, we suggest having students visit a leadership meeting.

1. Students visit a leadership meeting

To help give your teens a sense of how the church is run (session 5), have them attend one of the following: a council/session meeting, a meeting of the deacons, a meeting of the elders, or a meeting of the pastoral staff (if you wish, you can expand this to include the various committees that function within your church). If possible, divide up your class and have representatives attend different meetings. If that's not possible to schedule, a single meeting that all

attend is fine. Each student should complete his or her visit prior to session 5, which focuses on the leadership of the church. A form for students to complete during their visit is printed on page 31 of the student book. The form can be torn from the book, brought to the meeting, and later returned to class during session 5 for discussion.

Contact your pastor for the best time for students to visit a meeting for, say, an hour or so. The purpose of the visit is to give students a sense of the work done by the elders and deacons and pastor. Should your students be attending a single meeting, you will want to accompany them. See session 5 and page 36 of this leader's guide for more details. *Note:* If this visit isn't possible, a video of a portion of a leadership meeting or an "in class" interview of leaders is suggested (see p. 37 for details).

2. Students visit a worship service of a local congregation

Choose a service that is somewhat different in style and content from your own (perhaps a Roman Catholic mass or a charismatic service). This could be done at any time throughout the course. It will take a bit of extra work to arrange but the visit could well be one of the highlights of the course for your students. See page 29 of the student book for a form to guide the visit. See session 2 and page 19 of this leader's guide for more details.

3. Students plan and implement a worship service.

In session 2, students plan a worship service for their congregation. Refining and actually presenting that service is an option that will strongly affirm the contributions your students can make to worship services throughout the year. If you and the class (possibly with the broader participation of the entire youth group) decide to do this, you'll need to schedule at least two or three additional one-hour sessions for fleshing out the plans and for practicing. See session 2 and pages 17-23 of this leader's guide for more details, including a complete article from *Reformed Worship* entitled "Reinventing the Youth Service."

Other group activities—such as service projects—are mentioned in the "extensions" at the end of each session.

Scheduling Guests

As mentioned earlier, inviting a number of guests from your congregation to your sessions should dramatically increase the impact of this course on your students. See individual sessions for details about whom to invite and what their roles should be. With the exception of session 3, the guests are part of the optional procedures. In session 3, which includes inviting guests as part of a regular step, alternate procedures for doing without guests are suggested.

If you're going to invite guests to any of your sessions, you'd be wise to begin your planning now, calling people well in advance of the date you'd like them to attend your class. You should also give them information about the session and how they fit into it. The list below will get you started. You probably won't want or be able to invite all the guests we've indicated, so make your choices carefully. No guests are suggested for session 1. Other sessions and our recommended guests are as follows:

Session 2: Worshiping Together

Invite two or three of the following: worship committee members, praise team members, liturgist, organist or other musicians, pastor, or others involved in leading worship. These people will help your group plan a worship service. Their advice will be especially valuable if you're thinking about refining and implementing your plans into an actual worship service for your congregation. See step 1 for details.

Session 3: Caring Counts!

Invite two or more church members who have received special forms of caring from the congregation. Also invite two or more members who attempt to give special care to persons in the church or community. These guests will briefly tell their stories to the class. Options are offered should you be unable to invite these persons to your class. See step 1 for details.

Session 4: Reaching Out

Invite a member of your church's evangelism committee or persons who have served on various outreach programs in your congregation. The evangelism committee member will serve as a resource person to help student teams dig up evidence of outreach to the community. The persons who have served on outreach programs are part of an alternative procedure designed to inform the class about the mission efforts of the congregation. See step 3 for details.

Session 5: Running the Church

Invite your pastor, an elder, and a deacon whom the class can interview to get an idea of their tasks. They can also serve as advisors for writing a recommendation to the council/session. See "pre-session" and step 4 for details.

Session 6: Growing in Our Faith

Invite the following guests to be interviewed about the impact of baptism, instruction, profession of faith, and the Lord's Supper on their faith: parents and a child who was recently baptized; a young person who recently made profession of faith; an elderly person who is enthusiastic about the benefits of church education; a young person who recently began taking communion; your pastor. See steps 2 and 3 for details.

Summary of the Sessions

- **Session 1: Catching the Vision**
  Using our church's mission/vision statements, we write a newspaper ad that includes several of our church's most positive attributes. We stage interviews of members of the church in Acts 2 to learn what a church should be and can do. Then we complete statements that reflect our personal hopes for our church. We close by offering prayers for our church.

- **Session 2: Worshiping Together**
  We organize into a "worship planning team" and discuss the purpose of worship, using Revelation 7:9-12. We agree on an overall theme and supporting Scripture for our worship service. Then we work in subcommittees to plan a specific part of a worship service. We learn about ways we can use our gifts in our congregation's worship, and we close with a brief time of worship.

- **Session 3: Caring Counts!**
  We listen to the stories of people who were cared for by members of our church or who care for others in special ways. From 1 Corinthians 12 we discover that a healthy church needs and uses all of its members. In small groups we draw body outlines and fill in the outlines with ideas for caring. As individuals we assess our own interests and abilities, then write an "action statement" telling how we might show love and care to others. We close by sharing our action statements and praying for each other.

- **Session 4: Reaching Out**
  We share stories of challenges and difficult tasks that we've faced. Then we look at the task Christ gave to his disciples and form teams to dig up evidence on the ways our church reaches out to its community and to the world. Next we write a personal "great

commission" and are challenged to commit to a specific act of witnessing. We close by praying for each other.

- **Session 5: Running the Church**

  We list some of the traits of good leaders we've known and then use Scripture to examine the quality of servanthood. Using our observation of a church meeting, we describe the duties of various church leaders and draw an organizational chart of our congregation. We draft a recommendation (with grounds) to be sent to the appropriate leadership group of our church. With an eye to the future, we describe jobs in our church that will prepare us for future leadership positions. We close with a prayer for the leaders of our church.

- **Session 6: Growing in Our Faith**

  We make a group poster that reflects the "secret" of spiritual growth. Then, working in small groups, we explore four ways the church helps us grow as Christians. Next we review what steps are taken in our church to prepare for professing our faith, and we assess our own readiness to take those steps. We close by reading a prayer from Scripture.

An extra seventh session is outlined on page 48. It focuses on the idea that we are on a *lifelong* spiritual journey.

As with any prepared curriculum, you'll naturally want to adapt our teaching/learning strategies to your own situation. For example, you may find that your group needs more time than we estimated for a given activity. Or you may not have a full sixty minutes of class time each week. Or you may be more comfortable using your own approach rather than one we've suggested. Be flexible—consider this a resource, not a recipe.

We also invite you to contact the editors of this course with your questions or comments. Please call 1-800-333-8300 and ask for an editor of *Discover Your Church,* or e-mail us at editors@crcpublications.org.

Thank you.
CRC Publications staff

Session 1

Catching the Vision

Session Focus
To be an effective church, we need to understand who we are now and what God is calling us to be.

Scripture
Acts 2:42-47

Session Goals
* to describe what our church is and does, as we see it
* to describe what the church is and does, according to Scripture
* to describe our church as it could be
* to see ourselves as playing an important role in shaping our church

Session at a Glance
Step 1: Using our church's mission/vision statements, we write a newspaper ad that includes several of our church's most positive attributes. (20 minutes)

Step 2: We stage an interview with a member of the church described in Acts 2 to see how the Bible describes what a church should be and do. (20 minutes)

Step 3: We complete statements that reflect our personal hopes for our church. (5-10 minutes)

Step 4: We offer prayers for our church to close the session. (5 minutes)

Materials, Guests
1. student book (this session uses pp. 2-5)
2. pens or pencils
3. Bibles
4. big sheets of paper or newsprint, brightly colored markers, masking tape
5. mission and vision statements of your congregation (if available), printed on newsprint large enough for everyone to read
6. (optional) brochures, current ads, or other statements describing your church
7. (optional) snack

Session Background
So what does a church look like when it's actually doing its job of discipling the nations (Matt. 28:18-20)?

Where can we get some idea, some vision of what we want our church to be like?

In Acts 2:42-47 we see the New Testament church freshly crystallizing out of the joyous explosion of God's love sparked by Pentecost. The rush of the Holy Spirit's outpouring begins the outward push of the gospel into the whole world. Three thousand are added to the church in a single day. That number keeps growing (v. 47). The church grows in quality as well as quantity. The power of the Holy Spirit allows these believers to overcome the confines of their own self-centeredness and materialism. Their love for their Lord and for each other weaves them into a genuine community of faith—into the family of God. Wow! Can our church look anything like that? What does God need to do to make it so? What can *we* do? Those thoughts lead us to the heart of this first session: What does our Lord want our congregation to become?

A Solid Foundation

Verse 42 tells us that this new community of believers is firmly anchored in the teaching of the apostles. It's the gospel that binds them together in true fellowship—not their love of sports or their pursuit of gain or self-fulfillment. They continue to meet together daily (v. 46). And "with glad and sincere hearts [they] praise God. . . . " Their fellowship is a spiritual one. But it expresses itself in very concrete ways. Verse 42 lists two of them: the breaking of bread and prayer.

The breaking of bread may well have included celebrating the Lord's Supper. But it extends beyond that. Verse 46 tells us, "They broke bread in their homes and ate together with glad and sincere hearts." In those days, even more than today, showing hospitality, sharing meals, and celebrating together were evidences of deep friendship. In their sharing of God's Word, feasting together, and praying together, the believers experience the joy of overcoming their natural isolation from each other. The Spirit molds them into the family of God.

Is God's Word at the center of your church's life? Hearing, learning, teaching, leading, confessing, witnessing, sharing, celebrating the gospel of Jesus Christ is what your church is all about. If it isn't, roll up your collective sleeves—you've got work to do!

One in the Spirit

The believers' awe at God's doings was so great that they all "were together and had everything in common" (v. 44). This does not mean that they adopted some kind of commun*ism* that wiped out private property. Verse 45 points out that people kept ownership of their possessions. They sold them voluntarily as the need arose, willingly sharing what God had given them. They "gave to anyone as he had need."

The joyous love that God's Spirit grants us for our Lord and for each other acts both as a glue and as a solvent. It makes us stick together and at the same time it loosens our grip on our possessions. It dissolves the inhibitors that keep us from finding our true unity in Christ.

In your church too, that same power of the Spirit can help overcome the obstacles of in-fighting, selfishness, greed, materialism, and needing to have things our way all the time. It also guards your church from finding community in something other than God's Word. Drinking buddies and gang members experience fellowship. But theirs is a twisted kind of community, not the kind that flows out of "glad and sincere hearts" (v. 46). People despise, fear, or merely tolerate the unity that forms around a hypodermic needle or the business end of a gun. Those are a far cry from the esteem the early church community enjoyed. It "enjoy[ed] the favor of all the people" (v. 47).

Throughout this session, reflect with your teens on what keeps your congregation members together. What's *their* secret?

Living Magnets

The believers described in Acts 2 are not introverts or snobs. They do not erect new walls or barriers that keep others out. Their unity attracts other people. And they gladly welcome and absorb these new folks into their fellowship (v. 47). Their internal growth as a community leads, in turn, to their external growth. The Spirit blesses them with both. Pray with your teens that God will bless, or continue to bless, your church with both as well.

So as we pray, what can we do? A church community that looks like the one we find in Acts 2 naturally fulfills the Lord's mission by

- devoting itself to gospel teaching (v. 42).
- enjoying genuine, loving fellowship (v. 42).
- sharing sacraments, resources, and prayer (v. 42).
- doing God's work (v. 43).
- generously providing for the needs of others (vv. 44-46).

- regularly joining together in worship (vv. 46-47).
- enjoying an excellent reputation in the world around them (v. 47).
- growing in numbers (v. 47).

Invite your class to join you in those happy tasks. You'll be examining them more carefully in the sessions that follow.

Bob De Moor
Theological Editor

1. Our Church—As We See It

One thing you'll want to do throughout this course is to help your kids know and feel they are an important and contributing part of the church. Watch for ways to do that whenever and however you can. Get off to good start today by letting the group see you're glad for this opportunity to be with them and to learn together about something you're excited about—your church. You may want to provide refreshments while you welcome them individually to the class.

When you're ready, hand out the student books and call attention to the title: *Discover Your Church and Why You Need Each Other.* Briefly explain that in the next seven weeks we're going to be doing exactly what the title says—in a way that will actually be fun at times and won't ever (you hope) put people to sleep. If you can be brief, this may be a good time to say a few sincere words about what your local church means to you—and how you'd like this short course to help each person get to know this church a little better.

Option

As an opening ice-breaker, have each person interview one other person, getting one ordinary fact about the person, one fact not everybody knows, and one thing he or she likes about your local church. Allow about one minute for each interview. Kids then present their facts to the whole class about the person they interviewed. As leader, welcome each person by name as he or she is introduced.

On page 2 in the student book is an opening exercise that will take students through a process somewhat similar to that undertaken by congregations who attempt to write a mission statement—only the kids will be designing an ad instead of writing a statement. Your students have been exposed to an enormous amount of advertising and often are able to analyze what works and what doesn't. Making an ad of their own can be fun and challenging.

After reading through the page, distribute large sheets of paper and markers to groups of three or four students (use pairs of students in smaller classes, or design a single ad together). Give the groups ten minutes to design their ad. Ask them to focus mostly on the content of their ads—they probably won't have time enough to fuss much with appearance and design.

Before the groups begin their work, display and read a copy of **your church's mission and/or vision statements** (make a large copy on newsprint prior to class or hand out a photocopy of the statements). Unfortunately, churches differ considerably on what they mean by a mission statement and a vision statement; generally speaking, however, a mission statement describes what the church is and what God wants it to do. A vision statement expresses the congregation's hopes of what the church can become in the near future.

You may also want to hand out brochures about your church, current ads, or any other existing materials that summarize what your church is all about. Tell the students they can use this information along with what they already know about their church to write their ad.

As the students work, wander around the room offering suggestions, helpful hints, and praise. If some groups need help getting started, ask questions like these:

- What about fellowship?
- What fun activities do we have that people should know about?
- What is it about our music that people might enjoy?
- What about worship? Do we value some particular aspect of our Sunday worship?
- What about education?
- What about helping people in need?

Provide masking tape so that each group can hang their ad in front of the group, and then let the students summarize what their group wrote and why. Be sure to provide lots of positive feedback as students are working to build their confidence for their presentation. If anyone is uncomfortable presenting, offer to help out by asking questions and letting him or her provide the answers. Encourage students to be brief and to the point.

After the groups have presented, briefly sum up the positive attributes set out in the ads (leave the ads on display until the end of the session). Tell the group that we've taken a look at our own views of what the church is like; next we'll look at an exciting church that the Bible describes.

Option

Designing an ad appeals to kids who like to write and draw. Consider giving an option to those students who enjoy dramatics, such as presenting a TV ad or a radio ad.

Option

Display your ads on the wall of the fellowship hall or another place in church next Sunday, or have a student volunteer design the ads using a word processing or desktop publishing program and print them in a church bulletin, newsletter, or on a bulletin board.

2. The Church—As the Bible Sees It

Ask a volunteer to read Acts 2:42-47 to the class (p. 3 in the student book). Then read over the directions for staging an interview between a cable news reporter and a member from the church described in the Scripture passage. Group students in pairs (if you have an odd number of students, have a reporter interview two church members at a time). To save time, you may want to decide which partner will be the reporter and which the church member.

Give students about five minutes for the interviews. Afterwards, sample their answers to the questions in the student book or to other questions that students made up.

Option

If someone in your church has a video camera and tripod, invite two or three students to do the interview for the rest of the class, have another student record the interview, and play it back for everyone to enjoy!

Option

If you'd prefer not to use the interview format, read the passage, then have kids work in pairs to list (on sheets of newsprint) the traits of the Acts 2 church. Give them one or two examples to get them started.

After the interviews, use questions like these for additional discussion:

- What do you like most about the church described in this passage?
- Is this New Testament church doing things you think our church ought to be doing?

Wrap up by comparing the attributes of the Acts 2 church (see session background) to the attributes that kids listed in their ads. Use a brightly colored marker to circle attributes on the students' ads that are similar to those listed in the passage in Acts.

3. Our Church—As We Want It to Be

Turn to page 4 of the student book and read the introductory paragraph. If your church has a mission statement and/or a vision statement or some other statement of purpose, now is the time to have everyone jot down those statements. Next, give group members a few minutes to reflect quietly and individually on their own personal feelings about your church and its future. Invite them to complete the three statements in their books:

- **I wish my church were more . . .**
- **If I could change one thing about my church it would be . . .**
- **The thing I hope most for my church is . . .**

Give your students space to work without feeling that others may be reading what they're writing. Sit at a distance and don't speak unless one of the students needs your help.

Invite students to share one of their responses if they would like to do so (no pressure!).

4. Our Church—As We Pray for It

Allow for a time of silence at the beginning of your closing prayer and explain that you'd like each of your students to ask God for one specific thing that they believe would help their church become more effective. After a time of silence, thank God for helping students sort through what makes a church effective, and ask God to help each and every student see that God has a place for them in shaping the church—right now *and* in the future!

Option

On page 5 of the student book are three expressions of what the church says about itself: Q&A 54 from the Heidelberg Catechism (the most ecumenical of all the Reformed catachisms and confessions of the Reformation period), sections 38 and 39 of *Our World Belongs to God* (a contemporary testimony of the Christian Reformed Church, 1986), and brief excerpts from "A Declaration of Faith" (a confessional statement adopted by the United Presbyterian Church U.S.A in 1977. In 1983, this denomination merged with the Presbyterian Church U.S. to form the Presbyterian Church U.S.A.). You may want to refer to these statements from time to time as you lead this course. All or of some of the statements could also be read aloud as a responsive reading to close each session.

Before students leave, have them sign their names on the inside front cover of their books. Collect the books and keep them until your next meeting.

Session Extensions

1. Writing a Second Ad

Toward the end of today's session, have your students regroup into their original ad-writing groups and write a new ad. Explain that this time they should write an ad describing their church as they would like it to be, based on what they learned today and on their personal vision for what would make their church closer to the church Jesus calls us to be. Display the ads in the same ways suggested for the option for step 1.

2. Follow-up on Student Comments

Session 5 offers students a chance to write a recommendation for consideration by the church council/session or other leadership groups in the church. Let them know today that they will have this opportunity later in the course. Their voices count and they will have an opportunity to be heard. Another option is simply to pass along their comments from this session, without waiting for session 5. Naturally, you'll need students' permission to do this.

Leader Preparation for Session 2

We don't want to nag you . . . but you will need to make some special arrangements for next week's session, at least if you're following our suggestions for inviting various guests to your sessions. For next time, make arrangements to invite two to four of the following people: worship committee members, praise team members, liturgist, organist or other musicians, pastor, or others involved in leading worship. Give these persons a copy of session 2 to read (it's OK to photocopy for this purpose), and let them know what you expect of them. Ask one of your guests to be prepared to talk to your students about how they can participate in the congregation's worship services.

You'll also need copies of a recent church bulletin, one for each student. The part you're interested in is the order of worship. Make photocopies if you can't get your hands on enough of the real things.

Continuing in the nagging vein, if you've not yet made arrangements for your students to visit a meeting involving church leaders (council/session, elders, deacons, pastoral staff), please do so soon. Students should make their visit before studying session 5 on church leadership. During their visit, students should complete the observation form on page 31 of the student book. The form can be torn from the book, brought to the meeting, and returned to class during session 5.

If possible, have different students attend different meetings; if this isn't practical, all students could attend a single meeting. In either case, be sure to talk to church leaders early enough so that they have time to plan as well. They may need to alter their agendas slightly should something confidential be up for discussion.

If attending a meeting isn't possible, you'll find alternate suggestions in session 5.

Session 2
Worshiping Together

Session Focus

Worship is the most important thing we do—in life and in church. When we worship with God's people, we gather together to meet with God, to praise and glorify God, to respond to God's Word and presence in a kind of dialogue with God. We can recognize the various parts that make up that dialogue, finding ways to incorporate our own gifts in meaningful and creative ways.

Scripture

Revelation 7:9-12; and a selection to be determined by students

Session Goals

- to tell why we worship
- to act as a worship planning team and design the basic outline of a worship service
- to be motivated to participate more fully in worship and to use our gifts to praise and worship God

Session at a Glance

Step 1: We organize into a "worship planning team" and discuss the purpose of worship, using Revelation 7:9-12. (5 minutes)

Step 2: We agree on a Scripture passage and an overall theme. (10 minutes)

Step 3: We identify the various elements of worship, then break into subcommittees to plan a specific part of a worship service. (20-25 minutes)

Step 4: We regroup and look at our overall order of worship. (10 minutes)

Step 5: We learn about ways that we can use our gifts in our congregation's worship services. (5 minutes)

Step 6: We close with a brief time of worship. (2-5 minutes)

Materials, Guests

1. student book (this session uses pp. 6-11)
2. pencils
3. Bibles
4. hymnal(s) your church uses, other hymnals with songs that kids like
5. copies of your church bulletin, one per student
6. list of Scripture and supporting Scripture on newsprint (see step 2)
7. notecards
8. (optional) Invite two or three of the following: worship committee members, praise team members, liturgist, organist or other musicians, pastor, others involved in leading worship

Session Background

It may seem like poor strategy to introduce your young people to worship this early on in the course. Worship doesn't usually rate very high on their list of favorite church activities. There's the urban myth of Junior being dragged to church by well-meaning parents. It's so hot in church that the varnish on the pews is melting onto clothes and perspiring skin. The pastor has been droning on relentlessly. Suddenly, after completing his fifth count of the organ pipes, Junior is appalled to hear the minister say that heaven will be one eternal, never-ending worship service. Junior has just been talked out of *any* desire to ever go there.

Be sure to empathize with your teens. Worship can be hard work. It doesn't always come easy. And it takes real commitment to God and to each other. They'll find that out as you put them to work planning a worship service themselves.

Glory to God in the Highest

Still, I can't think of a better way to summarize what the church is all about than to quote the very first Q&A of the Westminster Shorter Catechism:

Q. What is the chief end of man?
A. Man's chief end is to glorify God, and to enjoy him forever.

That terse introduction pops us right into the heart of biblical teaching about the church and worship. Worship is the most important thing we do in church because it's the most important thing we do, period. Revelation 7:9ff. shows us that everything else we do—from telling people the gospel to helping them with their earthly needs—we do for one goal. That goal is that we together may glorify God forever and ever—and not just us: "a great multitude that no one could count, from every nation, tribe, people and language, standing before the throne and in front of the Lamb . . . " (7:9).

God's glory is the reason the church exists because it's the reason we exist. We don't first of all go to church to be amused, entertained, encouraged, instructed, or energized. Some of these things should happen. But first and foremost we go to church to honor God. And the more we experience God there, the more we will *want* to worship and the more we will be built up together into the massive throng that one day assembles around God's throne. To glorify God is to *enjoy* God forever.

Nothing boring about that! John's vision shows a dynamic celebration by all God's people. They're dressed in white robes, symbolic of having been cleansed and made right with God. They're waving palm branches like we wave flags at a parade (v. 10). They're shouting at the top of their lungs (v. 10). And there are angels, four awesome creatures, and the elders, all milling around the pulpit and throwing themselves on the floor in adoration. This whole crowd is doing what comes naturally to those who live in the full presence of God: they reflect and radiate back God's own awesome splendor, beauty, perfection, power, and goodness. And because there's always more of God to discover and enjoy, our celebration will not get boring even when it lasts forever. Be sure to keep this image in mind as you work with your teens in planning worship that's truly God-directed. The first question that will probably pop into their minds—How can we make this service interesting for everybody?—is not the real question they should ask. Help them focus instead on God: How can we and our fellow believers bring to God the best we've got?

In Conversation

Notice who is being worshiped: "Salvation belongs to our God, who sits on the throne, and to the Lamb" (v. 10). Notice also who is doing the worshiping: "they who have come out of the great tribulation: they have washed their robes and made them white in the blood of the Lamb" (v. 14).

Here we see the conversation that happens in worship between God and believers. God invites us, welcomes us, speaks to us through the Word, strengthens our faith through the sacraments, and blesses us on our way. We, in turn, talk to God in words, songs, prayers, and deeds. We praise God for his greatness, thank him for his goodness, confess where we've failed God, and declare and demonstrate our desire to obey his Word. As is the case with all

of our family conversations, these are intertwined. We interact. We dialogue.

Our worship should allow for real dialogue. It should have a logical order that makes sure that what needs to be said is actually said. But that order also needs to be flexible so that it helps us express and meet the very real concerns and needs we have in the here and now. Help your teens to think through both of those. What structure underlies our worship plan? How can we shape that structure to allow for really meaningful conversation with our God?

Rich Rewards

We worship because God deserves our worship and because our worship matters to God. If we work hard at it together, then our worship will certainly benefit us as well. The author of Hebrews writes: "Let us consider how we may spur one another on toward love and good deeds. Let us not give up meeting together, as some are in the habit of doing, but let us encourage one another—and all the more as you see the Day approaching" (10:24-25). *Always* in our worship God has something to teach us, to tell us, to show us, and to hear from us. And *sometimes,* even when it's stuffy in church, God really does give us a glimpse of heaven . . . the real one . . . the one we really *do* want to go to.

Bob De Moor
Theological Editor

1. Why Worship?

Today we suggest you turn your class into a worship committee and have them plan a youth service. This "hands-on" approach will take kids into the elements of worship and help them see how they can play a part in the worship services of your congregation.

Please consider inviting several worship leaders to this session (see list on p. 14). You'll want to advise them ahead of time on what's expected of them: basically to act as "resource persons," to explain how they assemble a worship service, to give advice based on their experience, to ask questions that will help students understand their assigned task as worship planners. It's possible, of course, to have a good session without these worship leaders, but their presence will tell your students that their opinions matter to the people who plan worship in this congregation.

Start by explaining that today's session is about worship. Tell them that the group will act as a "worship planning team" and plan a youth service for your congregation. By the end of today's session you and your group will have the rough beginnings of a plan for such a service. If you sense that the plan has possibilities and your teens are interested enough to follow through, we encourage you to work with them (and possibly with your broader youth group and worship committee) to refine the plan and use it with the congregation as a youth service. For a wonderful resource that will help you do this simply and effectively, see "Reinventing the Youth Service" by Jane Vogel and Mary Sytsma (*Reformed Worship,* March 1999). The complete article is reprinted at the end of this session.

As you work through today's session, you may find yourself running out of time. Maybe it took longer to find a theme and supporting Scripture than the ten minutes we've allowed. Maybe the planning teams took longer to get into their tasks than anticipated. If this is the case, be open to extending your study of worship into another session.

Begin today by asking the group to think with you about why we bother to go to church and worship God. Why do we worship? To help answer this question, have the group turn to Revelation 7 in their Bibles. Explain that verses 9-12 describe worship that's taking place in heaven right now, around the throne of God. It's an awesome scene! Ask for a volunteer to read these verses aloud.

After the reading, let students suggest an answer to the question "Why worship God?" Affirm that the main reason we worship is to praise and glorify God simply because God is so great and awesome. God has done great things. God is totally deserving of our worship, our praise. We want to express our love and admiration. And, though this particular passage doesn't suggest this, we also worship in order to listen to God, to learn what God has to teach us. This is the dialogue idea that will be developed later in the session.

You may want to explain it this way: suppose Michael Jordan (or some other person of note) were coming to town and we were to have the honor of meeting him (or her). Think of how we would feel in this person's presence (awed, honored, humble, special!). Maybe we'd say something like, "I think you're the greatest basketball player ever. I love the way you slam-dunk. I remember when you . . . " (praise, recall, adoration). Though God is infinitely greater than any famous human we might ever meet, per-

haps this will give kids a sense of the mood and purpose of worship.

You may want to make some (brief) comments that show your awareness of the gap between what our worship should be (the Revelation passage) and what it sometimes is, especially for youth. Admit that, yes, we are sometimes bored by church. Yes, sometimes we go only because we have to. Yes, sometimes the gifts of young people are not used enough in worship. Let your students know that you (and your guests) will be listening for their ideas and opinions on how to change and improve worship in your church.

As your opening prayer of praise, ask the group to read verses 10 and 12 aloud, in unison:

Salvation belongs to our God,
who sits on the throne,
and to the Lamb.
Amen!
Praise and glory
and wisdom and thanks and honor
and power and strength
be to our God for ever and ever.
Amen!

Option

To save time, you may want to take a couple of minutes to explain the purpose of worship to the group, using the session background as your guide and omitting the rest of step 1.

Option

In place of the Scripture reading, distribute notecards and ask each student to complete this statement: "I worship God because . . . " Share answers with the group. Affirm all responses and emphasize that God is worthy of our worship. By our worship we praise and glorify God for all that God is and has done. And we listen to God and learn what God wants to teach us.

2. Selecting a Text and a Theme

Tell the class that the first thing most worship planners do is select a Scripture passage and a theme or idea that comes out of the passage. This can be hard and lengthy work, simply because there's so much material to choose from! If the group comes up blank, have some suggestions ready for their consideration (or offer these suggestions as starting points). Here's a short list of Scripture passages and themes that might appeal to early teens (please add your own ideas as well):

- Luke 11:11-32 (the prodigal son); theme: the forgiving love of God

- Matthew 14:22-33 (Peter walking on water); theme: learning to trust

- Luke 10:30-37 (the good Samaritan); theme: breaking down barriers

- Luke 12:16-21 (the rich fool); theme: being content with what we have

- James 2:14-17 (faith and works); theme: living out our faith

- Matthew 6:25-34 ("Do not worry"); theme: seeking God's kingdom

- Matthew 6:5-15 (Jesus teaches his disciples to pray); theme: how to pray

- Revelation 7:9-17 (the great multitude); theme: joyful worship

It will save some time if you have your list of Scripture passages and themes on newsprint, ready to go. Try to settle on a Scripture passage and theme as quickly as possible, making sure to give the kids a voice in the process.

Take time to read the chosen passage aloud, so that all groups have it in mind as they begin planning.

Option

Have your guests tell the group how they go about planning a worship service at your church. This will help take the session out of the theoretical and into reality. If your planners start at a somewhat different point, you may want to follow that model instead of step 2, above. Remember, though, that worship planning can get quite complex!

Given your time limits and this age group, you'll want to keep things simple.

3. Planning a Worship Service

Have the group turn to page 6 in their student books, where they'll find a generic "order of worship." Review this material with the group, pointing out the various parts of worship as you do so. As the small planning groups work, they'll be filling in this "order of worship" with the specifics from their own planning group.

Option

If you prefer to use your own church's order of worship rather than the one we've printed, supply your students with recent bulletins and use these in place of page 6. Students can work with this order of worship (rather than one we've provided) when they plan a specific part of the worship service.

Option

If you've invited worship leaders to this session, ask one of them to lead the group through the "order of worship," using page 6 of the student text or your church bulletin.

Take a moment to explain that we worship together with God's people. God is so great that we need *everyone* to praise God! And when we praise God *together*, we sense that we are a community—we encourage each other, we pray for each other, and so on. Comment that our worship is something like a talk or dialogue between God and the congregation: God speaks and the people respond. Point out a couple of places in the order of worship where this happens.

Option

Use the material on page 10—"Worship Talk"—to help the group understand how worship is like a dialogue. The kids can read the part of the people, you or one student can read the part of God.

To introduce the worship planning activity, read the general directions under "Planning a Worship Service" (p. 7), starting with the paragraph that begins, "OK, here's your chance to plan a worship service."

Next, turn to pages 7-9, and assign kids to one of five groups, according to which part of the order of worship they're working on:

- Gathering to Worship
- Confessing Our Sin
- Hearing God's Word
- Responding to God's Word
- Parting to Serve

If your class is smaller than ten students (two per group), deal with it by leaving some parts of the worship service unassigned (they can be developed later, if you refine this plan into an actual worship service). Another approach is to assign more than one part of the worship service to a single group.

The task of each group is explained on pages 7-9 of the student book, and some guidelines are given. If you've invited worship leaders to the class, ask them to circulate among the groups and offer help as needed.

Provide the small groups with hymnals, Bibles, copies of your church bulletin, and anything else you think might be useful. Encourage the students to be creative and to design a time of worship that will be truly meaningful to them.

Most of the tasks will be simply making selections about songs, prayers, and how to do various things; however, here and there groups may find time to write a short call to worship or a closing benediction or even a brief responsive or unison reading.

Keep an eye on the clock as the small groups work. Save enough time (at least 15 minutes) to regroup and summarize the plan and to conclude the session. It's OK if some groups don't finish their assignment. The idea is to provide some hands-on experience, however limited, in putting together a worship service. Details can be fleshed out later, if and when you produce an actual youth service (in this regard, be careful not to make any promises that you can't keep).

Please point out that the sacraments of baptism and the Lord's Supper are often part of the order of worship. Mainly to save time, we've left them out of today's exercise; however, session 6 includes a discussion of both sacraments as means of nurturing our faith.

4. Putting It All Together

Reserve some time for the small groups to report on their work and to assemble a reasonably complete order of worship. As the groups report, have the students write their ideas on the order of worship (p. 6). Don't get bogged down in debating whether something is appropriate or not. Do make a point of noting at what points young people can be involved in elements of the service.

If you have access to an overhead projector, use it to record the group's overall plan (or use a large sheet of newsprint or your board).

5. Using Our Gifts in Worship

In many ways this is the most important part of the session because it assures students that their congregation needs them and wants them to participate in its worship services. If your pastor or worship leader is present, he or she could lead this section and say clearly to everyone present: "Here's where we can use your gifts in our regular worship service. Here's where you can help others worship God."

Page 11 of the student book may help you out here. It lists a number of possibilities for early teens to be involved in your worship service. First, as the instructions suggest, have students check those items that are possibilities in your congregation (please add other items that pertain to your local situation as well). Then ask them to circle any items that they'd like to do or learn to do for their congregation.

Follow up this last item by distributing notecards and asking each person to jot down one or more of the things he or she circled and is most willing to do or learn how to do. Explain that you'll be giving the cards to your worship committee (or other appropriate group) for follow-up. Have the kids sign the cards, then collect them. It will be very important for you to ask those to whom you give the cards to contact the kids who filled them out and to look for places where their gifts can be used in the worship services.

Be sensitive to group members who do not wish to be involved in any of the activities you've listed. Assure them they are still valuable members of the congregation, that their participation in worship with their families and the larger church family is sorely needed, and that they can do less obvious things like pray for the sick, contribute to the offering, sing, and so on.

Option

Since the notecards are going to those who plan your worship service, have the students use one side to express their opinion about how the worship services at their church could be improved and made more effective. This activity would also give kids something to write who don't want to volunteer for a job at this time.

6. Closing

Try to create an atmosphere of worship in whatever time you have left in the session. Here are a few suggestions to chose from:

- Light a few candles, sit in a circle on the floor, sing a familiar song (maybe one from the order of worship the kids put together), and pray. Prayers could be voluntary completions of the statement "God, I praise you for . . . " Close the prayer yourself by asking that each person present may experience the blessings and wonder of worship. Also ask specifically that each student will discover a gift that he or she can use to enhance the worship of your local church.
- Once again, read the passage from Revelation 7 with which you began the session (see step 1).
- Read (in unison) one of the faith statements from page 5 of the student book.

Session Extensions

1. Banner

Some of your students may be interested in creating a banner depicting some aspect of worship. The banner could be done outside of class or worked on during part of each session. If you have a person or committee in charge of banners for your church, it would be great to involve them in this project. Here are some suggested themes for the banner:

- Our chief end is to glorify God, and to enjoy him forever (question 1 of the Westminster Shorter Catechism)
- Revelation 7:9
- Postures of worship
- Music in worship

- Texts from Psalm 117 or 150
- Prayer in worship

Materials needed for the banner will vary, depending on how elaborate you want it to be. Here's a starter list:

- large piece of felt, at least 4' x 5'
- numerous scraps of colorful cloth
- sequins, glitter, paints, cord, and so on to decorate banner

2. Other Worship Projects

If designing a banner doesn't appeal to your group, discuss another project you could undertake that would help your students deal with worship themes. For instance, students could decide to work on a dramatic reading for worship, design a series of bulletin covers, or practice a choral or instrumental piece for an upcoming service.

3. Field Trip

Plan a field trip to a local church whose liturgy differs substantially from that of your congregation (for example, observe a Roman Catholic mass or a charismatic service). A simple form is provided for this on page 29 at the back of the student book. The form can be torn from the book and brought to the worship service. Discuss the experience immediately afterward. Don't wait a week, or much of the impact will be lost.

Leader Preparation for Session 3

For next time, we suggest you invite the following guests to your class:

- two or more church members who have received special forms of caring from the congregation.
- two or more church members who attempt to give special care to persons in your church or community.

Hearing the stories these guests tell is an important part of session 3. But we do provide a "no guest, no fuss" option if guests are in short supply.

Session 5 on church leadership is rapidly approaching. Before it arrives, we hope you are arranging for your students to visit a meeting involving church leaders. An observation form is provided on page 31 at the back of the student book. The form can be torn out, completed at the meeting, and returned for discussion during session 5.

Reinventing the Youth Service

discipling young people in a way that benefits the whole congregation

Jane Vogel and Mary Sytsma

If you've ever suffered through trying to organize an unfocused group of teenagers into a cohesive team of worship leaders, you may have asked yourself, "Why are we doing this?" That's the way we felt when we started working with our church youth group eight years ago. It took us a while to figure out how the youth service we had inherited fit in with the rest of the youth ministry program. Were we only going through the motions each year because "We've always done it that way"?

After several years of trial and error, the light finally dawned: worship planning arises out of the same principles we use for the rest of our youth ministry.

Principles for Planning Youth-Led Worship

Focus on Process, Not Product

We are in the *process* of training leaders throughout all our programming, including worship planning. This wasn't always the case. In the past, we did a worship service from the top down: we directed; the kids followed. We focused on presenting a polished "program" featuring the teenagers rather than on equipping the students to glorify God.

The catalyst for changing from performance to real worship was the realization that the Word must be the focus of every part of the process. At every step of the way—in choosing music, designing artwork, structuring prayer—we refer to the passage as a guide. As a result, the steps of planning, preparing, and leading have become as important to the students' spiritual growth as the final one hour spent in the sanctuary.

Prepare So That Everyone Can Be Involved

Second, we work to involve all students in using the gifts they have. Not every student is ready to stand in front of the congregation, but every student has something to contribute to the body. When we focus on ministering *with,* not just *to,* the students, we discover the importance of both identifying and valuing their individual gifts. As a result, a youth service may look very different from one year to the next.

Since we're not good at everything that goes into helping kids plan and lead a worship service, we have found that involving other members of the congregation benefits us—we can't and don't have to do it all. It benefits the students too, because they get to know other adults in the congregation. And it benefits the other adults we involve as they share the joy of working with the youth.

Some of these adults come to our youth group meetings when we plan the worship service. The choral music director, for instance, works with us during the first part of each planning meeting. The students do most of the work on the banner during regular meeting times, so the artist who works with them comes for that time. Other adults do behind-the-scenes work: writing a drama, for example.

Teamwork among the pastor, youth leaders, and students is a crucial part of this process. We work together to choose a Scripture passage for the service. Usually we focus on a specific passage rather than a theme, partly because our pastor prefers preaching a text rather than a theme, but also because this is one more way to draw the students back to the centrality of the Word.

Remember the Goals

From our days of doing a youth service because "we've always done one," we have moved to working with a clear set of goals that we communicate to leaders and students alike:

To use students' gifts to glorify God and edify the body.

To let students know they are the church *now.*

To provide opportunity for another kind of "profession of faith."

Nuts & Bolts—The Mechanics of Worship Planning with Youth

Choose a Text

Sometimes the text for the service comes from a retreat or Bible study the students want to explore further. Other times the pastor or a member of the congregation suggests a text. However, we always involve both students and pastor in the decision. We dedicate four youth group meetings

Sample Worship-Planning Bible Study

Structuring the Worship Service

1. Brainstorm elements of worship (prayer, confession, praise, etc.) as a whole group.
2. Use the passage, Colossians 2:6-7, to structure the elements. Talk the full group through the passage, helping students think of where the elements identified above might fit. Below is a sample with ideas; what the students come up with may be different.

Scripture: Colossians 2:6-7

"Just as you received Christ Jesus as Lord . . ."
—students' faith stories
—prayer of thanks for those who encouraged our faith
—songs

. . . "continue to live in him, rooted . . ."
—Apostles' Creed

. . . "built up" . . .
(this is the communal aspect)
—prayer for needs of congregation members
—faith stories about God's working through his church
—reports on youth group activities

. . . "strengthened in the faith as you were taught . . ."
—Scripture and sermon

. . . "overflowing with thankfulness."
—offering
—prayers of thanks
—singing
—testimonies

3. Personal challenge:
Ask kids to think about where their faith story might fit into this structure and encourage them to consider whether they might have a story or testimony to share.
4. Group brainstorming of music for each section of the worship.

---

to planning and preparing to lead the youth service, so we need to settle on a text at least a month before the date of the service (our group meets every Sunday night).

Study the Passage as a Group

We used to skip this part until we realized that by skipping it, we were not communicating the truth that the Word is the central part of worship. Now our first "worship planning" meeting is a Bible study. (See the box "Sample Worship Planning Bible Study.")

Discuss Why We Do What We Do in Worship

When we talk through principles of worship, we accomplish two things. First, we educate students. Second, we provide a common ground for making choices about what elements to include in the service. For example, when we talk with students about worship as a dialogue, we help them see how that concept affects the order of worship. As we discuss the difference between corporate worship and private devotions, we see students challenging each other to think about more than personal taste.

Have Students Form Planning Groups

Planning groups may change from year to year, depending on the gifts of the students. We try to have something that everyone can do so that there are no bystanders, and we encourage students to consider where they are needed, not just what area appeals to them most.

Those who plan an element of the service do not necessarily lead that element during the service. A student who is uncomfortable speaking in public may be very good at writing a litany for others to lead.

Work in Planning Teams

Here's where planning with the students will fall flat without advance preparation. We provide specific directions for each planning group and assign an adult or student leader to keep the group on task. (See the box "Sample Worship Planning Teams" for an example.) We think through whatever supplies the group may need and have them on hand.

Often, much of what students develop in their planning teams grows out of their experiences in the youth group throughout the year. For example, our group has developed a tradition of how we handle prayer requests: As people share their requests (or items for praise), one or two designated students write each request on a separate sheet of paper. When they have recorded all the requests, they pass the papers around the circle. Each group member takes one

Sample Order of Worship Developed by the Group

Gathering to Worship
Choral Call to Worship: *"As We Gather"* Renew 6
God's Greeting
Hymn: *"I Will Sing of the Mercies of the Lord"* *PsH 169, TWC 30*

Confessing Our Need
Early in human history our first parents listened to the intruder's voice. They fell for Satan's lie and sinned.

Apart from grace, we prove each day that we are guilty of rebellion too. We fail to thank God. We break God's laws. We ignore our tasks. We are separated from our Creator, from our neighbor, and from all that God has made.

God did not turn his back on his creation but provided his Son to reconcile the world to himself.

—based on the Contemporary Testimony *Our World Belongs to God*, section 14, 15

Psalm 40: *"I Waited Patiently for God"* *PsH 40*
stanza 1, Young people; stanza 2, Congregation

Hearing the Word
Scripture Reading: *Colossians 2:6-7*
[read by a student]
"Just as you received Christ Jesus as Lord . . ."
Prayer of Thanksgiving for those who were agents of God's grace in our lives.
[led by students, who asked the congregation to mention people who had been influential in their faith lives, then offered prayers of thanks for those people]

"Continue to live in him . . ."

"Rooted . . ."
Dramatic Reading: *The Apostles' Creed*
[by students]

Hymn: *"How Firm a Foundation"* *PsH 500, PH 361, RL 172, TH 94, TWC 612*

"Built up . . ."
Faith Story
[told by a student]

Prayer
[led by a student]

"Strengthened as you were taught . . ."
Sermon
Faith challenge to young believers
[by a student]

Choral Response: *"You Are My All in All,"* Songs for Worship and Celebration *220 (Word)*

"Overflowing with thankfulness . . ."
Offering Prayer
[led by a student]

Offering

Offertory
[by students]

Hymn: *"Now Thank We All Our God"* *PsH 454, PH 555, RL 61, SFL 33, TH 98, TWC 374*

Prayer of Gratitude
[led by students]

Serving in the World
Parting Blessing

Parting Song: *"We Are Marching in the Light of God"* *(from South Africa;* Renew! *306,* Voices United *646,* With One Voice *650)*

---

or more requests and prays them aloud. The students have sometimes chosen to employ a similar method when they lead the congregational prayer.

Practice, Practice, Practice
Worship is not a performance, but we offer our best. And students are more comfortable when they know where to sit, when to stand, and so on.

How the Congregation Benefits
When youth are involved in leading worship, the congregation sees the covenant affirmed. When other members of the congregation see teenagers owning the faith and giving back to the body of Christ, they will realize that young people are real contributors to the life of the church. Often this realization leads to a fuller involvement of youth, not only in "regular" worship services, but also in other areas of ministry.

Sample Worship Planning Teams

Planning Teams

Students choose to work in one of the following teams over the course of three youth group meetings.

Music

Using the master list of songs brainstormed by the whole group, this group should compile a "short list" of songs for both the congregation and the group to sing in the service. The group should work with the structure developed earlier to fit the music in appropriately. Other songbooks will also be available. **The short list should be finalized at the first meeting so the group can begin practicing the songs at the next meeting.**

Art

This group should work on preliminary banner and bulletin cover designs based on the passage at the first meeting. They should assign people to purchase supplies before the next meeting.

Prayer

This group has two jobs: (1) To determine where and what kinds of prayer they want in the service:

—Do they want separate prayers relating to each of the topical categories (being rooted, built-up communally, thanksgiving)?

—How do they want those prayers structured?

—Ask for prayer requests from the congregation and have different members of the group pray for them?

—Write out a prayer and have one or more group members read it?

—Other ideas

(2) To write out any prayers if they choose to have some written.

This could be done in a future meeting or assigned to willing volunteers to do by the next meeting. They should agree on structure: for example, will there be multiple readers? How will the prayer be organized? (ACTS? Some other way?)

Note: Members of the prayer planning group do *not* necessarily have to lead the prayers during the service, although they may if they wish. Other willing volunteers from the rest of the group can be solicited if desired.

Faith Stories/Testimonies

This group will be composed of kids willing to share their faith stories/testimonies. Work with students to determine where in the service those stories would best fit and help them develop their stories.

Communal Statement of Faith

This group will select or develop an appropriate way for the congregation to express our communal faith. Possibilities include:

—presenting the Nicene Creed as a readers' theater

—expanding the Apostles' Creed with personal, contemporary material

Jane Vogel and Mary Sytsma are youth leaders at Wheaton Christian Reformed Church, Wheaton, Illinois. sjvogel@mcs.com; dmsyts@mcs.com

This article is reprinted from *Reformed Worship* 51, March 1999, by permission of CRC Publications.

The hymns suggested in this sample order of worship were selected from the most recent editions of the *Psalter Hymnal* (PsH), *Presbyterian Hymnal* (PH), *Rejoice in the Lord* (RL), *Songs for LiFE* (SFL), *Trinity Hymnal* (TH), and *The Worshiping Church* (TWC).

Session 3
Caring Counts!

Session Focus
Christ intends the church to be a caring community. It's the body of Christ, made up of many different parts, each part necessary, each part contributing to the functioning of the body, each part linked to and caring for the other parts.

Scripture
1 Corinthians 12:12-22, 25-31

Session Goals
- to discover practical ways people in our church care for one another
- to understand how acting on the biblical image of the church as Christ's body means using our gifts to care for each other
- to list specific ways (and, optionally, to act on some of those ways) that we can help care for others in our congregation

Session at a Glance
Step 1: We listen to the stories of people who share personal experiences about how they were cared for by members of our church or how they attempt to care for others in the church or community. (15 minutes)

Step 2: By studying the body image passage in 1 Corinthians 12, we discover that a healthy church needs and uses all of its members. (10 minutes)

Step 3: In small groups we draw body outlines and fill the outlines with ideas for ways to show others in the church that we care about them. (15 minutes)

Step 4: As individuals we assess our own interests and abilities, then write an "action statement" telling how we might show love and care to others in our church community. (10 minutes)

Step 5: We close by sharing our action statements in small groups and by praying for each other. (5 minutes)

Materials, Guests
1. student books (this session uses pp.12-15)
2. pens or pencils
3. Bibles
4. sheets of paper large enough to use for drawing an outline of a student (three or four)
5. crayons or washable markers, masking tape
6. (optional guests) two or more church members who have received special forms of caring from the congregation; two or more members who attempt to give special care to persons in church or community (see step 1)

Session Background
The Bible presents us with lots of images for the church: the salt of the earth, the light of the world, the bride of Christ, the people of God. But in 1 Corinthians 12, Paul gives us an image of the church that homes in on how Christ intends us to be a living, caring community. Paul calls the church "the body of Christ." It's a living organism governed by one head: Christ himself. It's animated by one Spirit. And it's tied together by shared needs and a shared fulfillment of those needs.

Pushed to the Fringe
In this passage Paul tries to correct a specific problem that the Corinthian church experienced. It's not that this congregation sat idle or lifeless. In fact, they were incredibly busy—hyperactive, really. Some members were over-eager to show their spirituality and their giftedness. They turned worship into a chaotic mess because too many Spirit-filled people were talking at once, or babbling in tongues, or vying for everyone else's attention (vv. 27-30). And they were more interested in using their gifts for their own self-advancement than for helping others. As a result, many other people felt that they were on the fringe. Comparing themselves to the elite insiders, they felt that they didn't belong. They became discouraged—they saw themselves as being not nearly spiritual enough. They felt excluded, unappreciated, and unimportant. Sound familiar?

We often face the same problem today. Young people aren't immune to it either. Some of them want to be front and center in church. Demonstrating their gifts makes them feel good. And good for them! But their "success" can easily stroke their ego too much. It can make them look down on others. Other young people are apathetic or aloof. They don't really see that they belong. They doubt that they really matter to anyone else. What can they contribute that really matters? So they distance themselves and try to find fulfillment elsewhere.

For these reasons Paul puts the image of a living organism front and center. "The body is a unit, though it is made up of many parts; and though all its parts are many, they form one body" (v. 12).

The first point Paul makes is that all members belong—regardless of their gifts. Since baptism incorporates all of us into Christ's body and we all "drink" of the Spirit (v. 13), we belong together. We're all "in." Regardless of what we can do, we all matter because we belong to Christ. Unlike the social networks young people tend to develop, in church they belong, regardless of the clothes they wear, the stuff they have, or who they hang out with. They're family. They matter. End of story. Be sure to emphasize this point throughout this session.

Doing Our Part

Paul directs his second point to the discouraged, apathetic crowd. Just because they don't have the same gifts or do the same things as some of the others, that doesn't mean they don't belong. And it doesn't mean either that their contribution is unimportant (vv. 14-20). True, the hand may do a lot more intricate, complex, and visible tasks than the foot. Feet we use to stand, walk, and kick stuff around with. But the hand we use to paint masterpieces, build jet planes, and tickle the ivories—altogether much more interesting stuff. So some people tend to withdraw because they can't do the fancy stuff. They feel unimportant.

That's why Paul points out how important *all* the gifts that God gives us are—as long as they're used to build up the body of Christ. If the body were made up only of eyes, Paul argues, then we couldn't hear anything. That's no good! If the church were only made up of preachers, then it would collapse. Nobody would unlock the building, welcome the people, run the programs, care for the needy, and so on. There isn't a single job in church that's not important. A church needs all of its gifts and all of its members. The church needs *you!* So lend a hand . . . or a foot, or . . .

Interdependent

Next Paul points to those with over-inflated egos. Don't think you're so gifted that you don't need the others, he warns (vv. 21-26). An eye or head may think it's all-important. And maybe it is. But so are the other parts of the body. Separated from the other parts of the body, the eye dies and can't see a thing. The rest of the body is indispensable to the head. It can be ever so smart, but without a beating heart supporting it, it's toast.

That's an important point for us to remember in a culture that thrives on independence. Our young people are bombarded with messages that tell them to be autonomous, self-reliant, masters of their own fate, answerable to nobody but themselves. But the Bible clearly teaches that we cannot and should not be independent—ever. If our cells were independent we'd be nothing more than a puddle of amoebas. If our cells were all just parasites, they would all starve and die. It's the mutual *inter*dependence of our cells that allows complex organisms to thrive—they all contribute and they all depend on each other.

In church that's no different. Paul points to the mutual interdependence that ties us together as the body of Christ. We need each other. That's why the Spirit has distributed Christ's good gifts. There are no superstars in the church of Christ. We all belong. We all can contribute something important. And we all need each other.

Paul gives another reason why we should cool it when we overestimate our own value in the church. He writes, "When one part suffers, every part suffers with it; if one part is honored, every part rejoices with it" (v. 16). Every part of the body hurts when one of its members hurts. When I snap a collarbone in a skiing accident, I don't prance down the hill rejoicing about how good the rest of my body feels. My hand supports my collarbone because it's connected to it and to the pain it bears. My legs walk slowly and carefully because it senses the hurt that jarring causes. In the same way, we can't be a part of the body of Christ and not feel the suffering and pain of our fellow members. We can't help caring about them. We can't shut out their grief or poverty. We just *have* to help them. And if they're hell-bound in their lifestyle, then we simply *have* to pull them back into God's ways. The love of Christ within us makes us naturally reach out to soothe the hurt, fill the need, and lead the way back to Christ.

Love Is the Glue

Paul concludes the chapter by clearing up a possible misunderstanding. The fact that every person is equally important to the body does not mean that all the tasks in the church are on the same level. There are shades of difference. Nothing's wrong with developing gifts or cultivating new ones. In fact, Paul encourages it: "Eagerly desire the greater gifts" (v. 31). Be of as much use to Christ's body as you can be. So keep working on it.

But the conclusion of this chapter doesn't end Paul's discussion on meeting each other's needs. He devotes the entire next chapter to describe the highest gift of all: the one that all believers possess, the one that truly ties them together right on into God's good eternity. It's the gift of love. True self-sacrificing love is God's good gift to us and in us. It shows itself in a kind, generous, compassionate, caring, willing, serving attitude to the others. It's the real glue that binds us together. We take our cue from Calvary. It's the love Christ poured out on us on Pentecost. So encourage your young people to love each other. Then they'll look after each other. They belong, whether they're seven or seventeen or seventy.

Bob DeMoor
Theological Editor

1. Caring for Each Other

Plan at least a week in advance for this session by inviting two or more members of your congregation to tell the class how they have been cared for by other members. For example, you could ask a young person who's been mentored by an older person in the congregation, perhaps in preparation for profession of faith. Or ask someone who's had an accident or been ill to tell how the prayers and visits of the congregation helped him or her. Maybe a student in your class can tell about a time when a church member brought in a meal because Mom or Dad was sick. Or perhaps someone who's experienced a death of a loved one can tell how the congregation helped during that sad experience.

You may also want to invite a deacon to tell (briefly) how the congregation attempts to care for persons in need from the church and the community. Or invite some caregivers, such as a couple of youth group members who performed "random acts of kindness," someone involved in a Stephen's ministry, a tutor, a prayer-chain member, a faithful writer of cards, a visitor to the sick, or others involved in various forms of caregiving in your community. Please try to include at least one young person in your list of caregivers. That's a very important way to remind your kids that they can be actively involved in the life of the church.

Depending on how many guests you've invited, establish a time limit (perhaps a minute or two each for multiple guests) and explain the purpose of their visit.

Encourage guests to tell a little story about their experience (more than "Someone brought my family a meal when I was sick" but not a detailed account of the illness or the meal).

Have your guests present their stories to the entire group. Before they begin, ask the students to record (for each story) how the church shows it cares (provide paper or note cards). Invite them to ask questions after each presentation, if they wish.

After all the presentations, quickly summarize some of the ways that care is given and received in your congregation. You may want to mention some ways that have not been covered by your guests.

If they're willing, have your guests stay on to be part of the discussion and small group work.

Option

If your class is large, students could divide into small groups of two to four each, interview a guest, then present their findings to the whole group.

Option

If you have a hard time finding people willing to attend your class to share their stories, you could ask them if they would write a paragraph or two about their experience (and then have students read them aloud for each other) or record their stories on cassette or video prior to the class. If you still have a hard time identifying people, talk to your pastor, deacons, or elders, and ask them to share some real-life (though perhaps anonymous) stories about how church members have cared for each other.

Option

No time for the above? OK, here's a "no guest, no fuss" approach. Draw a large outline of a church on your board or on a huge sheet of paper. Caption the drawing: *Our Idea of a Caring Church.* On the outline write several sentence starters like these:

- People at church would treat me as if . . .
- Whenever I had a problem, I'd be able to . . .
- When I wanted to help out at church, I could . . .
- Adults would show me that I'm an important church member by . . .

- I could help by . . .

Supply markers and let kids mill around the poster and complete the sentences. They can add their own ideas without using the sentence starters, if they wish.

2. Body Care Bible Study

Explain that the apostle Paul said that the church was like a human body. In fact, the church is often called "the body of Christ." Have the group turn to page 12 and take turns reading the verses from 1 Corinthians 12. Then work through the four questions together. Guidelines follow.

1. How is the church like a human body?

Be sure to give the group time to think this through. Have them jot down responses in their student book as they are given. Some possible responses include the following:

- Both a church and a human body have many parts (members), each different, each with an important job to do.
- In a human body and in the church, all the parts (members) are necessary and important. Be sure to mention that this very definitely includes junior high kids!
- Just as all the parts of a human body make up one body, so all the members of a church are one body.
- When one part of a human body is hurt, all the rest of the body suffers with it. When one member of the church is hurting, the rest of the church also hurts with him or her. You could illustrate this by using the example of the broken collar bone—see the session background.
- In a human body an eye cannot say to a hand, "I don't need you!" So in the church, one member cannot say to another, "Hey, you're not as important as I am. Who needs you, anyway?"
- Just as we take good care of all the parts of our bodies, so church members ought to take good care of each member.

2. What does this Bible passage say to you about your place and job in the church? Try finishing these three "I" statements:

- "I . . .
- "I . . .
- "I . . .

The idea here is to personalize some of the conclusions gathered under question 1. Have volunteers read their statements aloud. Here are a few sample responses:
"I'm an important part of the church."
"I count!"
"I belong.
"I can help care for others in the church."
"I have gifts that God can use to help my church."

3. Why should people in a church care about each other?

Return to the body image as you discuss this. Why should an arm "care" about a leg? An eye about an ear? A foot about a hand? Because they're all part of one body. What happens to one part affects the others.

4. There's a lot of variety in the church. Different members have different gifts and use them in different ways. So what make us *one* body? What holds us together?

Call attention to the first few verses of our passage. Note what we have in common: one Spirit, one baptism, one Lord. You can also point out that the chapter that follows our passage—1 Corinthians 13—describes the "glue" that holds the different parts of Christ's body, the church, together. That glue is love.

3. We Care

Tell the group that you know they have lots of ideas about how people their age can show they care for others in the church community. That's what we're going to work on in this part of our session.

Divide into small groups of three to four students. Give each group a sheet of newsprint that's about three feet wide by six feet long (large enough to hold the body outline of one of your students). Tape together several sheets of newsprint, if necessary, or use a large sheet of cardboard or whatever else will do the job. Also give each group a box of crayons or washable markers.

Tell the groups they will be given ten minutes to draw an outline of one of their group members on the large sheet you've given each group and then fill it with written statements about how they can care for others in the church community. Add a little fun and competition by offering some corny prizes for the most interesting body outline, the most unusual caring idea, and so on.

The groups will have to quickly choose one of their members to be the model for the body outline. Caution those who are doing the tracing to be careful not to get the crayon or washable marker on the clothing of the person being outlined.

When everyone understands the task, give a signal and let the fun begin! After ten minutes (or less time if you wish), have each group present its drawing, read its suggestions for showing care to church members, and attach the drawing to the wall (with masking tape or poster putty) where everyone can see it.

Note: If your class is very small, make a single body outline and together fill it with suggestions for caring.

4. I Care

Comment that we've just listed a whole bunch of things we can do to show others in the congregation that we care about them. Obviously, each person can't do all of these things (that's the advantage of having lots of different people and gifts in the church!). Explain that in this part of the session, we're going to narrow the focus to ask how each of us *as individuals* can use our gifts and abilities to care for others. Ask the group to turn to pages 14-15 in their student books, and read the introductory comments aloud.

Just as the parts of a human body need each other, we need each other in the church. We all belong here. God has given each of us certain personalities, certain things we like to do, certain gifts or abilities to use to help care for others in our church community. Each of us has something to contribute.

How can you personally show that you care? A good place to start is to ask yourself what kind of person you are. For example, are you friendly, shy, talkative, quiet, active, cheerful, helpful? Think too about what kind of things you enjoy doing. For example, maybe you like to read or play a trumpet or shoot baskets or bake cookies or write or draw or talk to people or cheer people up or show others how to do something or pray for people or sing or dance or whatever.

Think about these things. Then try writing a couple of sentences that describe you, what you like to do, and how you could use your gifts or abilities to help care for others in your church community.

Read through a couple of the sample statements from pages 14-15 (or use your own statements), then allow a few minutes for students to complete their own "action

statements." Class members could also take an idea from the body outlines that they developed in the previous step.

5. Closing

Give everyone a chance to share his or her statement with others. Perhaps the best setting for this is not the whole group but small groups of two to four students each. This sharing should be voluntary. Be sure to let students know they have the right to say "I pass" when they're invited to share.

Thank the students for writing their statements, and warmly invite them to put their statements into action. To encourage this, have students pray for each other in their small groups. They can ask for God's help in putting their action statements into practice. Even if students haven't shared their statements, group members can still pray for each other, simply asking God to help them care for others in their church community.

Option

For an alternate closing, have each person jot down (on a small slip of paper) one gift or ability that they think God has given them to use in the church. They needn't sign their names. Pass around a container and collect all the slips. Then pass around the container again and ask the students to draw a slip at random. Open the prayer yourself, saying something like, "Thank you, God, for the gifts of each person here today. Our gifts are different, yet each one is important to the church. We thank you for the gift of . . ." (name the gift on the slip you've drawn, then the person next to you thanks God for the gift he's drawn, and so on, until all the gifts are identified).

Another possibility is simply to read in unison one of the testimonies of the church on page 5 of the student book.

Session Extensions

1. A Group Care Project

If you have the time and students are interested, you may want to plan and carry out a group project of caring. Here are some examples:

- visit an elderly person who can't make it to church anymore

- visit a child in the hospital
- organize a paint party or yard party
- help a family move
- collect food for a food pantry
- visit a nursing home
- help to serve a supper for family night at church

You may want to contact a deacon or elder from your church for specific needs in the church or community. Once you've decided on what to do, be sure that the group is involved in planning the details as well as carrying out the project. You don't want this to be *your* project. The whole class should own it and participate fully.

2. Improvisation

This step could be used in place of or in addition to step 3. Provide props and basic costumes (hospital gown, hats, handkerchiefs, canes, crutches, etc.) and have your students improvise (act out on the spot with little preparation) reactions to people with needs in the church. Ask one small group to identify a crisis or need and decide how to demonstrate it. Ask another small group to "respond on the spot" in way that shows the kind of caring and interdependence talked about in the Bible passage. For example, one group may decide to act out a grieving family; the other group must decide (spontaneously) how to respond. To make the improvisations more challenging, you could have students use actions only instead of words to show a need and respond.

Another approach is to provide story starters like the following and let the actors the complete the stories.

- Your best friend's dad is badly hurt in a traffic accident. Your friend calls you, tearfully tells you the bad news, and asks you to come to the hospital. When you get there, your friend and his family are sitting in the hospital waiting room. Your friend's dad is undergoing emergency surgery.
- One of the kids in your youth group tells you that her mom and dad got divorced. She and her mom moved across town, so she doesn't see her old friends much anymore. You sense that she's lonely and depressed.
- You're at the mall and you see a kid who used to be in your youth group at church. You haven't seen him around for a while. Now he's hanging around with some kids you know are really bad characters. In fact, you heard that a couple of them have been caught shoplifting right here in the mall. You go over to say hi and see how he's doing.

Make up your own story-starters that reflect situations your kids actually experience.

3. Resource for Leaders

Today's session introduced students to the process of identifying and using their gifts. If you'd like to pursue this idea in more detail, you'll want to check out *Discover Your Gifts and Learn How to Use Them* by Ruth Vander Zee (CRC Publications). The course uses a gift questionnaire and in-class tasks to help students identify and use fourteen specific spiritual gifts (6 sessions, junior high, high school).

Leader Preparation for Session 4

For next time, you'll need the following:
- a recent bulletin (one or two copies)
- your church directory (one or two copies)
- any printed information that's given to visitors (one copy)
- any printed information about your church's missionaries (one copy)
- any printed information about your church's outreach to the community (one copy)

You may also want to invite a member of your church's evangelism committee to the session, as well as others involved in your congregation's outreach to the community and world—see step 3 of session 4 for specific suggestions.

Here's a reminder to arrange to have your students visit a meeting involving church leaders (council/session, elders, deacons, pastoral staff). Try to arrange the visit before studying session 5 on church leadership. An observation form is provided on page 31 of the student book. Students may tear out the form, complete it during the visit, and return it to class for discussion during session 5.

Session 4
Reaching Out

Session Focus
When Christ met his disciples after his resurrection, he gave them a command and a promise that continues to shape the mission of the church and its members today.

Scripture
Matthew 28:16-20; Acts 1:8

Session Goals
- to explain the Great Commission and what it means for the church and for individual church members
- to describe how our congregation shares the good news with the community and the world at large
- to describe specific ways that young persons can witness
- to commit to doing one specific act of witnessing

Session at a Glance
Step 1: We share stories of challenges and difficult tasks that we've faced or will likely have to face. (5-10 minutes)

Step 2: We look at the task Christ gave to his disciples. (10 minutes)

Step 3: We form teams and dig up evidence on the ways our church reaches out to its community and to the world. (20-25 minutes)

Step 4: We write a personal "great commission" and are challenged to commit to a specific act of witnessing. Then we close by praying for each other. (10 minutes)

Materials, Guests
1. student books (this session uses pp. 16-19)
2. pens or pencils
3. large sheets of paper or newsprint, markers, masking tape
4. a recent bulletin (one or two copies)
5. your church directory (one or two copies)
6. any printed information that's given to visitors (one copy)
7. any printed information about your church's missionaries (one copy)
8. any printed information about your church's outreach to the community (one copy)
9. (optional guests) a member of your church's evangelism committee; various persons who have served on outreach projects (see step 3)

Session Background
You can find much of the context of today's passage in the student book at the beginning of session 4, "A Challenge from Christ." Be sure to consult that section as you prepare for this session.

Two Messages
Notice how carefully Matthew structures his account of the Lord's resurrection. He begins by recording the first links in the chain of witnesses to this cosmic event: the angel, Jesus himself, the women. . . . The chain ultimately stretches over two thousand years and across a very large ocean to us. And from us it will continue to spread to the teens we lead and through them again to others.

But Matthew tells us about the first links of another chain as well. It's the one begun by the Jewish religious leaders, pressed on the soldiers guarding Jesus' grave, reported to the governor, and "widely circulated amongst the Jews to this very day" (v. 15). It's the anti-gospel—the lie that Jesus never rose from the dead and that the good news of his resurrection is nothing but a farce. That story also continues to be told in our day and age.

Two chains have begun. The one tells the truth of the empty tomb and the risen Lord. The other tells the lie of a rotting corpse and a band of frauds. Why do these chains coexist? For how long? Which one will win? For the answer, refer back to Jesus' own explanation, recorded in Matthew 13:24-30 and 13:36-43.

Because of the many messages our teens receive through their headsets and TV cables, we adults may worry that the truth about Jesus is in grave danger of being drowned out. But that won't happen. Jesus himself reassures us as he reassured his ragtag band of followers: "All authority in heaven and on earth has been given to me" (v.18). If we think things look bleak for believers now, we should think back to conditions when the disciples met Jesus on that mountain! Such a small group of fishermen, traitors, and cowards! (Remember how they all ran out on their master?) And even they themselves doubted (v. 17)! But Jesus isn't worried. They won't have to fulfill their mission on their own steam.

The Mission

So what are the disciples supposed to do? They're supposed to counter the lies and baloney being spread by the religious leaders (vv. 11-15). They're supposed to "make disciples of all nations" (v. 19). That means spreading throughout the world the good news of Jesus' death and resurrection. And teaching people how to live their lives in that wondrous new reality. From now on, nothing will ever be the same. Not only the Jews, but all nations may now become God's covenant people. We may all become followers of Christ. God has given Jesus the whole she-bang—all authority in heaven and on earth. Jesus now has the right to lay claim to the whole creation. And he has the power to make it stick. All the disciples—and those who follow them—need to do is let people know this good news so they can live accordingly. To make sure that the eleven understand what making disciples means, Jesus clarifies it. The disciples are to teach them "to obey everything I have commanded you," he says (v. 20).

Confirming their teaching, they must also baptize the nations "in the name of the Father and of the Son and of the Holy Spirit" (v. 19). That means that they may do more than just *tell* people that they belong to God. They are given the authority of the triune God to *show* them as well.

To their marching orders Jesus attaches a promise: "Surely I am with you always, to the very end of the age" (v. 20). Go and do the work of spreading the good news, Jesus tells them. Incorporate the nations into the church. And in their work they'll meet Jesus. They'll experience his very real presence there with them—even though he's bodily up in heaven. He won't be there now and then. He'll be there for the duration. Right until the very end.

So many times in my ministry I've bumped into the truth of Jesus' promise. When I tell the story of Jesus' victory to those who don't know it, Jesus makes that story come alive for me as well. Seeing it again "for the first time" through the eyes of a seeker makes me meet Jesus all over again in a whole new and exciting and fresh way. Encourage your students to try it as well. It works. Rarely have my stumbling efforts been met by skepticism. Almost always the Holy Spirit has been there way before me, preparing the heart of the person to whom I'm telling the story. The more I've started telling Jesus' story—which is

my story as well—the less afraid I've become to tell it. Jesus' promise is true: "Surely I am with you always, to the very end of the age" (v.20).

Remember to follow through on Matthew's description of the gospel chain. The apostles began the work of spreading the gospel—Peter, then Paul. Then came evangelists like Timothy. Following them came the martyrs, the Church Fathers, priests and pastors and missionaries and parents and church school teachers. Bringing the gospel in word and in deed is the central mission of all of us. Peter tells us, "You are a chosen people, a royal priesthood, a holy nation, a people belonging to God, that you may declare the praises of him who called you out of darkness into his wonderful light" (1 Pet. 2:9).

The Power Source

Notice that the disciples did not immediately go out to spread the good news about Jesus' crucifixion, resurrection, and ascension. They did as Jesus told them. They waited in Jerusalem for the coming of God's Spirit. Under our own steam we could never accomplish the mind-boggling, worldwide mission Jesus gave us on that mountain. Acts 1:8 tells us that Jesus attached another promise besides the promise of his presence. "You will receive power when the Holy Spirit comes on you; and you will be my witnesses in Jerusalem, and in all Judea and Samaria, and to the ends of the earth."

The book of Acts demonstrates how on Pentecost the Holy Spirit begins to widen the circle. The church begins to spread. Three thousand are added to the number of believers in a single day through the Spirit's power. Pretty amazing! But Pentecost hasn't stopped. No way! That was only the beginning. Today in every country of the world many, many more thousands are becoming disciples of Jesus Christ. They're baptized into his church. Some of them are evangelized by missionaries in dramatic ways. Most aren't. Most become followers of Jesus through much more ordinary means: through a family member who passes the news along, through a neighbor or friend who invites them along to church, through a coworker who models a new way of living in this tired old world.

Maybe that's why Jesus gave the women such an ordinary greeting when he first met them on the road (v. 9). He can do incredible miracles in such ordinary ways. He can use ordinary people to do such extraordinary work. Even when they doubt and don't quite have their own spiritual house in order. Even when they're young and don't really have their act together yet. I guess that means he can also use the likes of you and me.

Bob De Moor
Theological Editor

1. Accepting the Challenge

Last time we suggested that students complete "action statements" detailing how they could personally show someone from the congregation or community that they care. You may want to begin by asking if anyone tried to put their action statement into practice. Be sure to encourage those who acted and those who did not.

Introduce today's topic—the Great Commission—by asking the group to think about challenges or tasks they've recently faced or must soon face. Give an example from your own life to get them thinking—maybe you've recently begun a new job or tried a new sport or volunteered to teach this class (talk about challenges!). For kids it might be the challenge of learning to play a new instrument, getting acquainted at a new school, joining a sports team, getting better grades, and so on.

Give the group a minute or two to think of something. Then ask for volunteers to share their challenge with the class. If your group is large, you could have kids share in small groups of two to four each.

Bridge to today's topic by commenting that we're going to focus on a huge challenge that Jesus gave the disciples—and all those who follow him, including us.

Option

Sports involving a high degree of risk are growing in appeal. Show the group some pictures you've gathered from magazines like *Sports Illustrated* of such things as rock climbing, hang gliding, snowboarding, and so on. Talk about why these extreme sports attract people today. While risking our lives for the fun of it is clearly not acceptable to Christians, people do respond to challenges of all kinds. Bridge to the idea that Christ challenges us to do something difficult and even risky: bringing the gospel to those around us.

2. Bible Study: A Challenge from Christ

Ask the group to turn to pages 16-17 of their student books. Read through the material under the heading "A Challenge from Christ," pausing when you come to the first "React!" activity. Give the students a few seconds to fill in the blanks:

As a disciple, how would you react to Jesus' presence?
__ rub your eyes and wonder if you were dreaming
__ bow down and worship
__ doubt if this stranger really was Jesus
__ be so shocked and amazed you wouldn't know what to do
__ be really calm and cool because you knew this would happen
__ other

Review responses, then continue reading to the next "React!" exercise:

As a disciple who has just heard these words . . .
• **How do you feel about this Great Commission or job that Jesus just handed you?**
• **What worries or concerns do you have about the job?**
• **What will help you get up the nerve to actually do the job?**

Take a minute to discuss each question before moving on to read "Mission Impossible?" to the class, pausing to let them fill in the missing words from Acts 1:8:

"But you will receive **power** when the **Holy Spirit** comes on you; and you will be my witnesses in Jerusalem, and in all Judea, and to the ends of the earth."

3. Digging up Evidence

In this part of the session, students will form three teams to dig up evidence that their church is indeed attempting to reach out to the community and to the world (see student book, p. 18). To prepare for this, have a table on which you've displayed the following items to help in the search:
• a recent bulletin (one or two copies)

- your church directory (one or two copies)
- any printed information that's given to visitors
- any printed information about your church's outreach to the community
- any printed information about your church's missionaries

Take a minute to read the directions (p. 18) to the group. Then devide into three teams of equal size. Each team should read it's own specific instructions (p. 18).

If you've invited a member of the evangelism committee to be present, ask him or her to be available to help any of the teams. He or she can circulate from group to group and offer help as needed.

Give each team a large sheet of newsprint on which to jot down a summary of what they found. Give each team a definite time limit (no more than 15 minutes), at the end of which they should display their summary and present it to the class.

One important thing to emphasize in each outreach area is the contributions that young people are making and can make.

Option

Another way to go on this section is to ask persons who have served on various outreach programs of your congregation to come to your class and briefly explain what they did (or are doing). Such persons could include the following:

- a young person who was part of a youth group outreach project
- a missionary on home service
- a member of the evangelism committee
- a Young Life leader at a local public school
- a volunteer at a local mission organization
- a community Bible study leader
- a young person involved in personal or friendship evangelism

This list is obviously not comprehensive. Include a variety of people (different ages, different kinds of service). Your class should see that there are many ways to reach out, and not all of them are formalized programs. Most of all, kids should get the message that outreach is something they can do, right now!

If you want to have a larger number of speakers but your time is limited, break your class up into small groups.

Option

Hold a mini "ministry fair" during this session by inviting various local and international ministries to come with their displays and just let your kids mingle informally with the guests. You could invite one or two of the guests to show a video about their ministry. If you go this route, be sure to ask the representatives to bring information about the volunteer opportunities they have for youth.

Option

Call one of the ministries your church supports with volunteers, prayer, or finances, and ask for an appropriate video to show your group.

4. My Great Commission

Page 19 of the student book offers a summary of the mission task of the church and its members from *Our World Belongs to God: A Contemporary Testimony.* You may want to ask for a volunteer to read it aloud.

Next, read through "My Great Commission," calling attention to the corporate and individual aspects of witnessing. Then invite all students to write their personal version of the Great Commission, imagining that Jesus is speaking directly to them and giving them a specific witnessing task to do. It should be something that challenges them yet is also realistic and "do-able." It should be something they are actually willing to commit to.

Conclude the session in one of these ways:

- Ask students to share their personal "great commission" with a partner and then pray for each other, asking the Spirit to help their partner with his or her witnessing task. Partners may also be challenged to hold each other accountable for doing what they said they would do (if so, allow time for checking with each other in next week's session).
- Ask for volunteers to share their personal "great commission" with the entire class. Then lead the group in prayer, asking the Spirit to help each group member with his or her witness task.
- Ask for a moment of silence, during which students may individually and silently pray for the Spirit's help in accomplishing the witnessing task they've decided to do.

Before students leave, remind them to bring their completed observation forms (from attending a church leadership meeting) to class next time.

Session Extensions

1. Getting Out There

Last week we suggested a "group care project" as a session extension. The focus was on showing care to someone in need from your church or community (see pp. 28-29 of this leader's guide for a full description). You may want to do one of the projects suggested in session 3, or try something different that your students suggest. Perhaps you can plan a project with a local ministry whose representative visited your class today (for example, spend a day helping out at a local urban ministry or do some work for Habitat for Humanity). Or you could plan to do some "random acts of kindness," such as passing out free balloons to kids at the mall, washing cars, and so on. You can hand out a card with information about your church to each person you help. Another possibility is to hold a twenty-four-hour fast for world hunger (contact your denomination's relief and development organization). Or talk with your denominational youth agency to get the latest information on service projects.

2. Personal Testimonies

Have you thought about challenging your students to write their personal statement of what Jesus means to them? While this may sound intimidating and even manipulative to some teens, it needn't be either. Explain that the statements don't have to be long and fancy. What matters is that the statements come from their hearts and express their honest feelings about Jesus Christ. If they feel somewhat unsure of their faith, their statements should reflect that uncertainty.

It's a huge step to go from writing a statement to sharing it with the group, but some of your teens may be ready to do this, if invited to do so in a very supportive and accepting environment. As leader, you may want to consult *Share Your Faith . . . and Keep Your Friends* (CRC Publications). This course is for high schoolers but has many suggestions for sharing "faith stories" that would be appropriate for younger students as well.

Leader Preparation for Session 5

Next week's session focuses on the leadership of the church. This means you've got one more week to arrange for your group to visit a council/session meeting, a meeting of the elders, a meeting of the deacons, or a pastoral staff meeting. Reporting on this will be part of session 5. However, if schedules have simply not allowed for these visits, a couple of alternatives are suggested.

Be sure students complete the observation form found on page 31 of their student books before session 5. They can tear the form from the book, complete it at the meeting, and bring it to next week's session for discussion.

Optional guests next time include two or three council members, a young person who is in a servant-leadership position, or a youth pastor. Please see steps 3 and 4 of session 5 to decide if you want to invite any of these guests. They are not essential to the session but could add to its impact.

You should also obtain a list of the names of your church's leaders: pastor(s), elders, deacons, committee chairpersons, and so on. You may also want to check your church's installation form for pastors, elders, and deacons for information regarding their duties. If possible, bring a copy of these forms to class.

Finally, we suggest you jot down the names and positions of your church's leaders, using notecards or a small slip of paper, one name per card.

Running the Church

Session Focus

The leaders in our church each have specific tasks and play important roles in decision-making. Each leader is called to model Jesus, who came not to be served but to serve. We can begin to develop our skills as servant leaders today, preparing ourselves for other leadership positions in the future.

Scripture

Matthew 20:25-28

Session Goals

- to describe the tasks and ministries of the various leaders in your church (pastor, elders, deacons, youth pastors, and so on)
- to describe the kind of leadership that Jesus modeled
- to draw an organizational chart of the church to see how each leader and committee functions within the entire congregation
- to design a recommendation to bring to an appropriate leadership group in the church
- to identify places in our church where youth can gain skills as servant leaders

Session at a Glance

Step 1: We list some of the traits of good leaders we've known. We use Scripture to examine the quality of servanthood, which Christ modeled and which he instructed all leaders to exhibit. (10 minutes)

Step 2: Using our observation of a church meeting, we describe the duties of various church leaders. (10 minutes)

Step 3: We ask who is the boss of the church, and we draw an organizational chart of our congregation. (10 minutes)

Step 4: We draft a recommendation (with grounds) to be sent to the appropriate leadership group of our church. (20 minutes)

Step 5: We identify servant-leader positions in our church that will prepare us for future leadership positions. We close with a prayer for the leaders of our church. (10 minutes)

Materials, Guests

1. student book (this session uses pp. 20-21 and 31)
2. pencils or pens
3. Bibles
4. large pieces of paper or newsprint, markers
5. notecards or small slips of paper with names and positions of church leaders, one name per card (for closing prayer; see step 4)
6. completed forms for "Observing Our Leaders in Action" (p. 31 of student book)
7. list of names of pastor(s), other staff, elders, deacons, committee chairpersons, and other church leaders
8. (optional guests) elder, deacon, pastor, or other staff to discuss their duties and to help draft recommendations; young person in servant-leadership position or youth leader

Session Background

Let's cut right to the chase, shall we? So who's the boss of *your* church? Is it the pastor? Is it the elders? Is it the membership? Is it the council or session? Is it an inner circle of long-time members? Is it some higher church assembly? Who? Is the church a democratic organization or is it a dictatorship? Who's got the real authority and the real clout?

To answer that question we should think back to our last session. Remember what Jesus said to his disciples before his ascension: "All authority in heaven and on earth has been given to me" (Matt. 28:18). That's pretty clear. Jesus is the God-appointed ruler of everything, including the church. That's why we call him our *Lord* as well as our Savior.

But Jesus is physically up in heaven and we're down here. So how do we know what he wants us to do? How does he provide us with the kind of day-to-day and week-to-week leadership that helps our church to grow and develop and mature and do its job? The Bible tells us that Jesus gives the church all kinds of leaders: leaders who help us know and follow the Bible; leaders who help us keep in step with the Spirit; leaders who help us become what our Lord wants us to be; leaders who help us do what Jesus wants us to do.

But Jesus doesn't just want any old leaders! He's very fussy about the kind of leaders that he wants to give to the church. They may have many different gifts, many different areas of expertise and responsibility. But they *must* all have one thing in common. As we'll see, in Matthew 20:25-28 he spells out clearly what that is.

An Unholy Rat Race

Jesus' teaching in this passage is prompted by a specific event that has just occurred. The mother of two of his disciples has just asked Jesus to favor them with the most important places in Jesus' kingdom. Like mother, like sons. They accompany Mom in her urgent plea (v. 20). They want those places of highest honor for themselves.

Jesus responds by suggesting that they cannot earn those places. They cannot take the cup of God's anger against the sins of humankind. Only Jesus can do that. No one else in Christ's kingdom has the right to any of it, including the honor it confers on those who enter in. Only Jesus has a right to it. The rest of us are there only because of his sheer, self-sacrificing grace.

Mom doesn't have a clue about this, of course. Nor do the lads, who stupidly imagine that they can carry the burden of sin right along with Jesus. Little do they know what truly awaits Jesus—and them—on Golgotha. Jesus points out that they will indeed taste a sip from that cup. But it won't make any difference. It's not Jesus' prerogative to decide who gets the places of honor. That's up to his Father and no one else.

Overhearing their request throws the other disciples into a rage. They understand full well that what James and John and Mom are asking would push *them* down a notch. That's the thing about the rat race. You get to the top by climbing on the back of the guy ahead of you. It's a mad scramble where a few get to the top by pushing the others down—way down.

In this context Jesus emphatically and explicitly denies that the kingdom of heaven will tolerate that kind of rat race. That may be the way this godless world works (v. 25). But there will be no "lording it" over others, or "exercising authority over them" (v. 25) in Jesus' eternal kingdom. While it's instinctive for us to head for the top, Jesus commands us to head for the bottom instead. He topples the pyramid of the human corporate structure on its head.

For Whom?

In this world people try to grasp leadership positions to gain power and prestige. They want to be leaders so that they can benefit themselves—either through their pocketbook, their image, or their over-inflated ego. But in church things must be different. There leaders must not serve themselves, they must serve everyone else! Jesus says, "Whoever wants to become great among you must be your servant, and whoever wants to be first must be your slave" (v. 27).

Imagine that! The most important people in church are those who do the work of servants and slaves. Those who willingly make themselves the least by serving others matter most. There are no bigshots in Jesus' kingdom. Leaders in church must always be *servant leaders*.

A Divine Example

The best example of that kind of leadership is Jesus himself: "The Son of Man did not come to be served, but to serve, and to give his life as a ransom for many" (v. 28). The only really important person in the kingdom of heaven, the only one who really deserves to receive all its honor and glory, came down from heaven *to be that kind of a servant*. He loved us so much that he emptied himself of all his godly glory and willingly died a slave's death on the cross—spit-streaked, scorned, stripped naked, flogged, and hung up to die in cursed agony. Our true leader willingly went through the cruel pain and utter humiliation of hell for us. And so he became the servant of us all—our souls' eternal ransom.

What gifts of leadership do your teens have? Will they use those gifts to benefit themselves? Do they have a servant's heart? Will they serve, or do they demand to be served? Will they willingly follow their Lord to the bottom? That's what this session is all about.

Bob De Moor
Theological Editor

Pre-Session Assignment

We hope that by this time your teens were able to visit a church meeting (council/session, elders, deacons, staff meeting, and so on) and take notes on the observation form we supplied on page 31 of the student book. Because students may forget to bring their observation forms to class, consider giving them a reminder postcard or phone call before today's session.

You'll be using the forms as background information in step 3. If you were unable to arrange a visit (we recognize that scheduling can be a problem), here are a couple of options to do instead.

Option

Videotape some of the more interesting moments from a church leader's meeting. You could do this yourself or have a couple of students from your class do it for you. Be sure to get buy-in from the groups you'll be taping and ask for their help in identifying an agenda item that illustrates their tasks and responsibilities. Then show the video segments during this session (using the fast-forward button liberally, if needed!).

Option

Invite several officebearers to your class (try for elders, deacons, and pastor or other staff). Have the students form small groups and interview them. Take a few minutes before the leaders arrive to brainstorm some questions that students could ask.

1. What Makes a Good Leader?

Begin today's session by telling the kids a little story about a leader (a pastor, a teacher, a mentor, an elder, a deacon, a parent) who made a difference in your life. It needn't be a long or dramatic story—just your heartfelt tribute to someone who helped you along on your spiritual journey.

Now ask the kids to think of a leader who made an impression on them. Have them get into groups of three or four and make a list of the qualities that made them admire these leaders. Give them two minutes to make a list (on sheets of newsprint). Then ask each group to tape its list to the wall and read the list aloud.

Comment that certainly many of the qualities the groups listed would also be desirable in those who are leaders in the church—our pastors, elders, deacons, teachers, youth leaders, and so on. Point out that Jesus really emphasized one quality in particular—a quality that he wanted all leaders of his people to have. Let the kids guess what it might be.

Distribute Bibles and have the group turn to Matthew 20:25-28. Ask someone to read aloud. Then ask questions like these:

- What's the key quality Jesus wanted leaders to have? (to be a servant leader)
- What's the opposite of a servant leader? How do you think such a person would act?
- How would a servant leader act?
- Jesus holds himself up as the model of a servant leader. What are some ways that Jesus acted as a servant?

Be sure to affirm that leaders in the church also need to be just that—they need to make decisions, take care of God's people, and run the church. But they do all these very important and necessary things with a humble, servant-like attitude.

Option

Compare the students' list of desirable qualities in leaders with those given by Paul in 1 Timothy 3:1-13. Even simply reading through the passage will give your class a sense of how carefully leaders of the church should be chosen. Much of the "servant" attitude is readily apparent in these verses as well: leaders must not rule for their own gain or be on a power trip. They must humbly follow their Lord and help all of us to follow Jesus as well.

2. The Leaders of Our Church

If your students paid a visit to a meeting of the council/session, deacon, elders, or pastoral staff, now is the time to listen to their reports. Bring the reports in as you talk about the duties of the leaders in your church. Use the headings on page 20 of the student book for jotting down information. Please note that room is left for adding "other" leadership positions, such as teachers, evangelists, youth pastors, minister of outreach, director of education, superintendents, worship director, and the like. You'll need to decide on how many leaders to include.

Ask the group to take out their completed form "Observing Our Leaders in Action." Keep the format open and flexible, allowing students to give their input and to raise whatever questions they might have. It will be helpful to the group if you use a large sheet of paper or your board to summarize the duties of each leadership position in your church.

We suggest you list the names of elders, deacons, pastoral staff, and committee chairpersons so that students sense that these are not just "positions" but real people in the church who give of their time and effort to be servant leaders of God's people. Give the names to students or have them find the names on the back of the bulletin or in the church directory.

You may want to refer the group to your church's forms for installing pastors, elders, and deacons, highlighting for them a few of the key duties of each office listed in the form. It may be more efficient, however, simply to supplement the students' responses with anything crucial that they neglected to mention.

3. How Our Church Is Run

Now that the group has simple job descriptions of major church leaders, it's time to look at how the church is organized. Begin by asking who they think is the boss or head of the church. Is it the pastor? The council/session? The elders? The deacons? The congregation? Nobody? If the group doesn't suggest "Jesus Christ," have them look up Colossians 1:18: "And he [Christ] is the head of the body, the church."

Explain that the church, with Jesus at its head, is run by certain leaders whom God has called to serve his people. Use a sheet of newsprint or your board or an overhead projector to sketch a diagram of how your church is organized. Have the students copy your diagram into their books on page 21. Because the lines of authority can differ from one congregation to another, you'll want to amend the following generic diagram as needed:

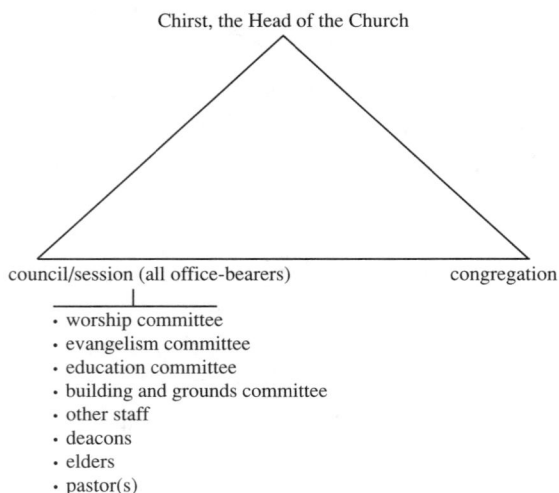

Chirst, the Head of the Church

council/session (all office-bearers)   congregation

- worship committee
- evangelism committee
- education committee
- building and grounds committee
- other staff
- deacons
- elders
- pastor(s)

When each person has copied your diagram, allow time for any questions the group may have. Also, you should point out a couple of features:

- All parts of the church recognize Christ as head of the church and exist to serve him.
- No one in the church, except Christ, is "above" the other members (that's why we use a triangle rather than a hierarchical, straight-line diagram).
- The congregation appoints the council/session and agrees to abide by its decisions. The council/session represents and serves the congregation.
- The officebearers (pastors, elders, deacons) serve the congregation and report to the council/session.
- The various committees of the church serve the congregation and report to the council/session. Elders (and sometimes deacons) are often represented on the committees.
- Individual congregations within a denomination are of equal influence. These congregations have agreed to delegate their authority to major assemblies called "synods" in some denominations, "general assemblies" in others.

Later in the session you and the students will have an opportunity to move a recommendation through the organizational structure of the church. Leave the organizational diagram on your board for use in the next step.

4. Decision-Making Time

Now that your organizational chart is complete, it's time to put it into practice. Divide into groups of two to four students each (or if the class has fewer than half-a-dozen students, stay in a single group). Explain that the task of each group is to think of a recommendation they would like to see carried out in their church. The recommendation might be for some sort of change or it might be simply a suggestion for something the church is not now doing but perhaps should be doing. Each group should come up with one recommendation and the reasons (grounds) the church should adopt this recommendation (how will it benefit the church?).

Suggest such general areas as worship, educational ministry, youth groups, building, outreach, and so on. Give the group an example. Suppose they would like to sing more contemporary songs in the worship service. Some grounds for this recommendation might be (a) contemporary songs would help attract young people to the services; (b) these songs have more meaningful messages for young people than some of the older, traditional songs; (c) many people in the congregation are not singing the traditional songs used in the worship service.

Tell the groups that this isn't just an exercise. Ask them to seriously consider what they would like to recommend and to come up with some good reasons (grounds) for the change. Then the whole group will decide if any of the recommendations suggested by the small groups should actually be sent to the appropriate church leaders for their consideration.

Give the groups ten minutes to write their recommendation and grounds (furnish large sheets of paper and markers for this activity). Then have the groups report. As each recommendation is given, talk about where on the organizational chain that idea could be brought for consideration, and how it might proceed from there. (For instance, the suggested change to more contemporary songs would probably be brought first to the worship committee, then to the pastor, then to the elders, and to the council or session.) Here are some other examples:

- Host a special weekend event to which young people could invite unchurched friends. (youth pastor—evangelism committee—council/session)
- Provide financial support for an outreach program for homeless youth that's run by a Christian agency in your community. (deacons—council/session)
- Build a basketball court for the youth group and neighborhood kids. (youth pastor or leader—building and grounds committee—church council)
- Begin a youth group for junior high kids. (education committee—elders—council/session—congregational meeting)
- Renovate the fellowship hall to make it accessible to people in wheelchairs. (building and grounds committee—council—congregational meeting)

After airing some of the ideas brought by the small groups, try to reach a concensus on which idea, if any, should actually be submitted to the appropriate leadership group for consideration. Perhaps one or two of your students could type up your recommendation and grounds, then meet with the pastor to discuss the recommendation and verify how it should be routed.

The value of this exercise is that it shows teens they have a voice in way the church is run, in the way it worships, in the programs it offers. While their suggestions may or may not be implemented, they will certainly be heard.

Option

Have a few experienced council members present during the above exercise so that they can move around the small groups answering questions and offering advice.

Option

If your students had a chance to visit a council or committee meeting, you could stage a mock council meeting, committee meeting, or congregational meeting to discuss one of the recommended items. If you do this, appoint a chair and a secretary to record the minutes and any motions that are discussed.

5. Servant Leaders Needed

Please take a couple of minutes to encourage teens to develop servant-leader skills by using their gifts in your church's worship and/or programs. Let them know that even the most routine service can help them become the church leaders of tomorrow—and can make an important contribution today. Talk with the group about ways in which they already serve and about ways in which they could serve. You'll want to share some of the following ideas:

- participate in the worship service (see p. 11 of the student book for a list of things teens can do in a worship service)
- assist a teacher in church school
- be a leader at this summer's vacation Bible school
- plan and implement a one-time special event that will serve members of your church or the community
- serve as a youth advisor on a church committee
- help plan and organize youth group activities

These are just a few suggestions that you and your students can supplement. All students should leave this session knowing they are important to the church and can make a real contribution.

Option

Invite a young person who is involved in a leadership position in your church to talk to your class about his or her experience and what he or she has learned. Or invite a youth pastor or youth leader to talk to the group about opportunities to serve and to develop servant-leadership skills.

Close today's session by praying for the leaders of your congregation. One way to do this is to write leaders' names and positions on notecards or small slips of paper, one name per card. Distribute the cards among your students and ask them to pray silently or aloud for the person on their card. Close the prayer time yourself by thanking God for the kids in your group and by asking that God would bless them as they follow Christ's example and serve God's people.

Session Extensions

1. Prayer Follow-up

Prayer for our church leaders is crucial. Your students can help by praying each day this week for the person mentioned on the notecards you distributed at the end of today's session. It would be especially meaningful if your students informed these leaders (via a note in the mail or a personal contact at church) that they are being prayed for.

2. Getting Our Feet Wet

Jesus washed his disciples' feet as an example of the kind of servant leaders he expected them to be (John 3:1-17). You may want to use that passage in addition to or instead of the passage suggested in step 1 (Matt. 20:25-28). Another possibility is to read the footwashing passage at the close of today's session. You could even try a footwashing ceremony in your classroom, if you're willing to tolerate a certain amount of giggling and joking that some kids won't be able to suppress. Have students do the footwashing in pairs, using dampened washcloths and towels that you provide.

3. Songs

If your students enjoy singing, you could close the session with Graham Kendrick's song "The Servant King" (*Maranatha! Music Praise Chorus Book,* Expanded Third Edition, 150). If your students know it already, sing it together. If they don't, you could ask musicians in your class to play and sing it through once or twice. Another option is "The Servant Song" (*Songs for LiFE,* 248).

Leader Preparation for Session 6

Next week's session focuses on four ways the church helps our faith grow: by baptism, by instruction, by profession of faith, and by the Lord's Supper. Please consider inviting the following special guests for small groups to interview in each of the four areas:

- parent(s) and a child who was recently baptized
- a young person who recently made profession of faith
- an elderly person who is enthusiastic about the benefits of church education
- a young person who recently began taking communion

Please see step 2 of session 6 for details. You may also want to invite your pastor or an elder to explain the process your congregation follows for profession of faith.

Again, bear in mind that these are optional guests. The session is very teachable without them. But their presence will help personalize these great benefits of the church for your teens. It definitely will be worth the extra effort of contacting these people and inviting them to your class.

One item you will need for next week is at least a six-foot section of white paper tablecloth on which students will write. Please see step 1 of session 6 for details.

Growing in Our Faith

Session Focus

The church plays a key role in nurturing our faith. God uses the church to instruct us in the way of salvation. God gives us the sacraments of baptism and the Lord's Supper to strengthen our faith. And God gives us the opportunity to confess his name before the congregation in a ceremony often called "profession of faith."

Scripture

Selections from Psalms 25 and 119; Proverbs 3:1-2, 5; Matthew 10:32-33; 28:19; Luke 22:19-20; John 15:5; Acts 16:29-31; 1 Corinthians 10:16-17; Galatians 5:22-23; 1 Timothy 4:12

Session Goals

- to be grateful for and want to participate in the various "faith-building" activities provided by our church
- to explain what God and parents promise in baptism
- to describe the role that instruction plays in deepening our faith
- to explain why we need to profess our faith and how doing so is related to baptism
- to list the benefits of taking communion
- to be encouraged to profess our faith and take communion with God's people

Session at a Glance

Step 1: We explore the "secret" of all spiritual growth and make a group poster that reflects that secret. (10-15 minutes)

Step 2: Working in four small groups, we explore four ways the church helps us grow as Christians. An optional part of this process is to interview several guests. We share the results of our small groups' work with the entire class. (30 minutes)

Step 3: We review what steps are taken in our church to profess our faith, and we assess our own readiness to take those steps. (10 minutes)

Step 4: We close this session and this course by reading a prayer from Scripture. (5 minutes)

Materials, Guests

1. student book (this session uses pp. 22-27)
2. pens or pencils
3. Bibles
4. large sheet of paper table cloth with the words from John 15:5 printed across the bottom
5. one brown marker, several green markers, several purple markers
6. information on the steps to make profession of faith
7. (optional guests) parent(s) and a child who was recently baptized; a young person who recently made profession of faith; an elderly person who is enthusiastic about the benefits of church education; a young person who recently began taking communion (see step 2); your pastor (see step 3).

Session Background

Can true faith "just sit there?" Is it enough for churches to have the right doctrines in the backs of their hymnals? Is it enough for people to be paper members of the church—to have their names on the membership rolls without ever darkening the door of the sanctuary? Can true believers spin their spiritual wheels for decade after decade without showing any real growth in their everyday lives? Those are critically important questions, for the church and for each person in your class.

Bearing Fruit

In John 15 Jesus teaches the disciples that true believers continue to grow in their faith. They bear the fruit of the Spirit. If they don't, then their faith isn't for real, it's counterfeit. It's dead. "I am the vine; you are the branches. If a man remains in me and I in him, he will bear much fruit; apart from me you can do nothing" (v. 5).

Let's back up a bit. Jesus has just predicted his suffering and death and the difficult reality of his imminent departure. To still the fears of his disciples about his departure, Jesus promises them another Counselor, the Spirit of truth (John 14:16-17). He promises them that through the Spirit, "I will come to you. Before long, the world will not see me anymore, but you will see me. Because I live, you also will live. On that day you will realize that I am in my Father, and you are in me, and I am in you" (John 14:18-20). It's to this theme of living in Jesus through the Holy Spirit that the Lord returns in John 15:1-17. The analogy

Jesus uses of the vine and its branches helps us to understand the life of faith in a number of important ways:

- *Only Jesus can give us eternal life.* In John 15 Jesus tells us, "I am the vine; you are the branches" (v. 5). It is the vine, and only the vine, that can give the branches life. You'll want to make this very concrete for the class. That's exactly the point of their baptism: "God reminds and assures us . . . that his covenant love saves us, that he washes away our guilt, gives us the Spirit, and expects our love in return" (*Our World Belongs to God,* section 40).

- *We will only have eternal life if we remain in Jesus.* It's not enough to get a new start with Christ. "If anyone does not remain in me, he is like a branch that is thrown away and withers . . ." (v. 6). Again, make this very concrete for the class. Faith is not a one-shot deal. Baptism isn't the end of our faith-life. It's the beginning. We need to keep on seeking Jesus and finding him in our worship, our fellowship, our learning, and our living. Without a life-long relationship with Jesus we wither and die. The Lord's Supper teaches that so clearly. We need food and drink every day again. We need Jesus every day or our spirits die. Section 40 of *Our World Belongs to God* continues: "We take this food gladly, announcing as we eat that Jesus is our life."

- *If we are alive in Jesus we will certainly bear fruit.* Our faith in Jesus will show in how we live and what we say. In John 15 Jesus points out that being in him results in love for him, love for each other, and obedience to Jesus' commands. We will show the same kind of love that Jesus showed us by dying on the cross. Our fruitful lives are not the reason why we are saved. Jesus is. We did nothing to deserve salvation. But being in the vine, in Christ, will necessarily result in a fruitful life. When we have Jesus' life coursing through our veins we can't do anything else!

Saying and Doing, Doing and Saying

Showing love for each other can take many forms. You can fill in the details with your class. But how do we show our love for Jesus? Paul writes, "If you confess with your mouth, 'Jesus is Lord,' and believe in your heart that God raised him from the dead, you will be saved. For it with your heart that you believe and are justified, and it is with your mouth that you confess and are saved" (Rom. 10:9-10).

Those who love Jesus talk about him. Simple as that. Those who believe in him confess his name. They tell each other about him. And they also tell those about him who do not yet know Jesus. That's what public profession is all about. In making public profession of our faith, we express our faith in Jesus and publicly commit ourselves to his service. That's an important event!

But again, a one-time profession isn't enough. Those who live in Christ will continue to confess his name throughout their lives. Every time we sing a hymn, join in a prayer, or say the Apostles' Creed, we're re-confessing our faith in Jesus. And every time we openly tell neighbors, fellow-workers, or classmates about Jesus, we're doing that too. There's an old Dutch saying that goes something like this: What fills our hearts pours out of our mouths. It's a good saying. Those who love Jesus can't stop talking about him. Their hearts overflow with his life-giving Word while their hands (and lives) pour out his abundant love on others.

The vine imagery Jesus uses in John 15 is a rich one. It ties together the various milestones of faith that we meet in this lesson:

- *Baptism* symbolizes our being grafted into Christ, the vine. Through the washing away of our sin and the gift of the Holy Spirit, our spiritual journey has begun.

- *Spiritual nurture* enables us to remain in Christ, the vine, and to continue to grow up in faith, hope, and love. The journey continues.

- *Public profession* shows everybody that as we grow in Jesus, the vine, we bear much fruit. We not only believe in our hearts but also confess with our mouth. And consistent with our profession, we show Christ's love in all our living. We don't walk our spiritual journey alone. We walk with each other.

- *The Lord's Supper* is an ongoing means of grace by which Jesus nourishes and feeds our faith through his Spirit. The life-blood of the vine flows to and through branches. We are truly one in the Spirit. We may experience already now along the road the celebration that awaits us at its end.

Given all these wonderful ways to "remain in the vine," there's no way true faith can "just sit there." Help your students catch that truth today, so that they—along with the rest of God's people—can move ahead on the journey.

Bob DeMoor
Theological Editor

1. The Secret of Spiritual Growth

If your students are submitting a recommendation to your pastor or elders or deacons or a committee (see last week's session), be sure to check on their progress today. Run any final statements by the class to insure ownership of the recommendation by the entire group, not just by you and those who drafted it. Continue to keep your students informed about the progress of their recommendation through official "channels," even if it means a call to them after this course is over.

For this exercise, you'll need a large rolled sheet of paper tablecloth, at least six feet long. At the bottom of the sheet write (or have a student write) these words from John 15:5: "I am the vine, you are the branches; if a man remains in me, he will bear much fruit." *Note:* You may want to change "man" to "person" and "he" to "he or she."

Begin by commenting briefly about how Christians of all ages want to grow spiritually and become better followers of Jesus. Ask kids what they think is the most important thing we have to do in order to grow spiritually. What do they think is the "secret" of spiritual growth? Commend all responses, such as "read your Bible more," "serve others," "pray more," "go to church," and so on.

Show the group your poster and read the Bible passage you've written at the bottom. Explain briefly that the real secret of becoming a better Christian is to "remain in Jesus," just as the branches of a grapevine have to remain attached to the main vine to grow fruit. (The comments in the session background section will help you explain this comparison in more detail to the students.) You will want to explain that it's the Holy Spirit who attaches us to Christ through the faith the Spirit gives us (see John 14:15ff.).

Gather the group around you and place the poster on the floor or on a table. Ask the students to illustrate the verse at the bottom of the poster, using their own names as part of the poster. They may want to do this in a straightforward way, sketching in a brown vine labeled "Jesus" and green branches labeled with their own names. Under their names they can use a purple marker to cluster the various fruits of the Spirit described in Galatians 5:22-23 (have the group look up this passage). Or they can do something a little more imaginative; for instance, instead of simply drawing a vine and branches, they can use the brown marker to write the word "Jesus" strung along in a wavy line resembling a vine. Their names could branch off the vine in the same, wavy pattern, using green markers. Instead of the "fruits of the Spirit," group members could write words that describe each person and his or her qualities or gifts.

Option

As an alternative to the poster, students could make a "living vine and branches," with some kids lying on the floor to make the vine, others becoming the branches, still others the fruit. The impact of being separated from the vine could be dramatically shown!

2. Four Faith-Builders

Divide the class into four groups of two to four students each. Distribute the student books and ask everyone to turn to pages 22-25, where they'll find four "faith builders" or ways the church nurtures our faith: baptism, instruction, profession of faith, communion. Assign one group to each faith builder. Groups should read through "What We Believe" on their assigned sheet, then jot down their response to the "Group Talk" questions. (Interview questions are optional—see page 45.) Call attention to the place where students can add their own questions about their topic, questions they may not know the answer to but would like to discuss later with the whole group.

Option

If you have fewer than eight students in your class, you can adapt the activity by dropping the "instruction" category and/or by reviewing the sheets as a single large group.

Allow about ten minutes for the groups to work, then reconvene and have each group summarize its answers to the "Group Talk" questions. Brief comments on the questions follow:

Baptism

- **What does the water in baptism tell us?**

It's a sign that God washes away our sins through the sacrifice of Christ on the cross. Take a moment to explain that baptism is also one of two sacraments in the church, and that sacraments are really "signs" that point us to certain truths God wants us to know. They are also guarantees or "seals" of God's promises to us.

- **What does God promise us in baptism? What do the parents promise?**

God says, "You are my child; now and forever I will be your God. You belong to me." This promise is part of God's covenant or agreement with believers and their families.

The parents say, "God, we promise to do our very best to raise this child to love you."

Note: You may want to add that in many churches, the congregation also makes a promise to love the child, to pray for him or her, and to encourage him or her to follow Jesus.

- **How does being baptized help us grow spiritually?**

We know that God chose us to be part of his family. We have God's promise to always stick with us, no matter what. And our parents and the congregation will help us get to know the Lord.

Instruction

- **List some ways the church has taught you about God.**

Students may mention church school, catechism classes, the worship service, songs, youth group activities, Bible studies, service projects, and so on. You may want to point out that we can learn about God through "hands on" experiences or through more formal classroom instruction. Do point out that we are never done learning about God—it's a lifelong process that continues long after we profess our faith and become adults.

- **Share one good thing that you've learned through a church-connected activity or class.**

This question gives students a chance to talk about that great retreat or that special youth convention or that really cool teacher or whatever else stands out in their short experience with "church education."

Profession of Faith

- **Why is it important to profess our faith before the congregation?**

Kids will quickly say, and rightly so, that the Bible clearly says we need to confess Jesus "with our mouth." In addition, when we profess our faith, we are claiming the promises God made to us in baptism. And when we profess our faith, we take our place with the rest of God's people and announce our willingness to share in the work and in the rewards of being part of the church.

- **How are baptism and profession of faith connected?**

Writing in *The Church Cares* (CRC Publications, 1987), Bill Lenters put it this way: "When you are baptized, God signs on the dotted line that you belong to him. And when God signs his name, he writes with indelible ink. It is stored in his memory forever. When you profess your faith, you sign *your* name on the dotted line. You say that you are pleased as can be to know Jesus and that you want to be his disciple. You are claiming the promises God made to you in baptism."

- **How do you think professing our faith helps it grow?**

As we've said, when we take a stand for God, we claim his promises for our own. We *know* that we belong to God and that God will never let us go. That's wonderfully comforting, especially when we go through hard times in our lives. Also, as we assume new responsibilities as confessing members of the church, our faith stretches and grows.

- **How do we know if we're ready to profess our faith?**

This is a key question that you should definitely address either here or in step 3 of the session. There's no easy answer, of course. The basic thing to communicate to your kids is that they should profess their faith when they sense the Spirit leading them to do so, when they want to let the world know that they love the Lord and want to serve him. They should *not* wait until every doubt or hesitation is gone, because for most of us, that never happens! Lenters puts it this way: "Don't let your age hold you back. Don't let what the other person does determine your decision. If you love the Lord Jesus, profess it now. The growing will come later. So will the growing pains. No matter. You are a part of the family of God. So sign on the dotted line, say that you claim God's promises made to you in baptism, and get yourself to the Lord's table. You belong."

Lord's Supper

- **What does the bread and wine in communion tell us?**

Review the definition of sacraments (see above) as you talk about this question. Then talk about how the broken bread reminds us of Christ's body, which was given for us, and how the wine (grape juice) reminds us of his shed blood. How much deeper you want to go than this simple explanation is your call. Note, for example, that the passage from 1 Corinthians 10 talks about "participation" in Christ's blood. The Heidelberg Catechism puts it this way: "We, through the Holy Spirit's work, share in [Christ's] true body and blood . . . to guarantee our share in his death and resurrection, and to unite us to him."

- **If you take communion, how has that helped your faith?**

This question will give those teens in your group who have already professed their faith a chance to say what taking the Lord's Supper means to them personally. The language needn't be theological but should simply be from the heart.

- **If you are looking forward to taking communion, how do you think doing so will help your faith grow?**

Again, let your group members express themselves. Then summarize any benefits they didn't mention: Communion draws us closer to God and to each other. It reminds us that in Christ, our sins are completely forgiven. As food nourishes our body, so communion nourishes our spiritual lives. Writing to young teens, Lenters puts it this way: "This is no magic act. The bread and wine contain no mysterious power, no spiritual drug that will send you off on some holy high. They are meant to refresh you on your journey of faith. Taking communion is more like taking a cool, refreshing swim on a hot day than like taking a shower because you are dirty. Jesus has already cleansed you with his forgiving love. The supper he provides is a joyful celebration of that cleansing. It refreshes you and reminds you that you are the Lord's. Who gets his supper? You do. It doesn't matter if you are thirteen or thirty—once you profess your faith, you are invited to the Lord's Supper."

You may want to conclude this step by asking students if there are other ways in which the church helps their faith grow. Students may mention the worship service (session 2), individual and group service projects such as those described in session 3, youth group meetings, retreats, youth conventions, and other activities.

Option

You'll notice that each sheet includes a section titled "Interview Questions." If you've decided to invite guests to your session, each group should meet with its guest (described below). Then, after reviewing the "What We Believe" section together, the group should go immediately to the interview questions. Notice that the section encourages students to make and ask their own questions of the guests.

After the interviews, have group members report to the class, focusing on one main question: How did the guest's experience with baptism, instruction, profession of faith, or communion help him or her grow spiritually?

We know it's something of a chore to get on the phone and arrange for these guests to visit your session today. But their presence will personalize the information-gathering activity and make it memorable for the students. And their role is not demanding: all they need do is let the kids ask them questions about their experience. Some suggestions for guests:

- **Baptism**

If possible, invite parents who are willing to take their recently baptized infant along to your class (it's OK if only one parent comes); or, as an alternative, ask a young person or an adult who's recently been baptized. Ask the guest(s) to bring along pictures or other mementos and objects to show the group (their baby's baptism gown, a baptism certificate, the bulletin from the service, and so on).

- **Instruction**

Look for an older member of the congregation who faithfully attends classes and/or small groups and who is enthusiastic about lifelong learning. Another possibility is a new convert who grew spiritually through a Bible study or some other educational program.

- **Profession of faith**

Ask a young person who has recently professed his or her faith. Check out class members first—the impact of having a fellow class member tell about his or her profession of faith could be considerable. Encourage the guest to bring photos, a certificate of profession of faith, or other mementos to show the group.

- **Communion**

It may be possible to use the same guest here as for the profession of faith interview. Again, if a person in your class takes communion and can describe his or her experience, you could have that person be the "guest" for this interview. Or ask another member who can describe a time when communion was especially meaningful to him or her.

Brief your guests on the goals of this lesson and prepare them for possible questions your students might ask. Invite your guests to stay for the remainder of the session and possibly to linger afterwards for refreshments so that your students have a little time to mingle informally and ask questions in a more relaxed environment.

If you invite guests, here are a couple of procedural alternatives you could consider:

- Have all the students interview all the guests (best for a small class).
- Have the students rotate from one guest to another, so that all the students hear all the guests. Set a definite time for how often the groups must rotate (about 5-7 minutes per guest should do it).

Option

If you can't invite guests to your classroom, consider the possibility of having students videotape a baptism or profession of faith or even part of a communion service. This tape could include a live interview with one or more of the persons involved. Obviously, this would have to be planned well in advance, and you might need to borrow camcorders from congregational members for the kids to use.

Another possibility is to assign groups of students to videotape the stories of the individuals described above before today's session.

3. Professing My Faith: Am I Ready?

The remainder of the session and the course focuses on profession of faith and uses pages 26-27 of the student book. Probably a good place to start is by taking students through the process followed by your congregation. Don't

assume that your students know what's expected of them. In fact, some of them may be holding back on making that commitment merely because they are hesitant to ask what they are supposed to do.

On page 26 we've provided a little template for your group to fill in. The first and last steps are already in place, and the group can fill in the rest right now, using information you've dug up and verified (with the pastor) before today's session. If someone in your class has already professed faith, draw on that person's experience to outline the basic steps your church requires, and talk about his or her experience in going through those steps. By the way, you can say that you have another step to add to the process, something the people who wrote the text didn't put in, something that's the most important step of the whole process: to go out and live what you confess you believe! This may help dispel the notion that profession of faith is something of a graduation ceremony, the end of a process. No way! It's an important milestone, a claiming of the promises made in baptism, but it's just one further step on the lifelong journey of faith.

Some of the kids in your group may be too shy to show a lot of interest during the meeting. But they may consider the information carefully in the privacy of their room after today's session. You may want to include the name and number of your pastor, the youth elder, and your home phone so that each student has someone to call to get more information, ask questions, or make a commitment.

Option

Have your pastor or youth elder explain the various steps and hang around after class to answer any questions one-on-one. He or she may also pass around copies of the kinds of questions that would be asked of them at profession of faith. Allow time for questions the students may have about the process or the form.

Continue by calling attention to the questionnaire printed under the heading "Am I Ready?" (p. 27). Give the group several minutes of quiet time to complete the questionnaire and add up their numbers (if time is short, the students can complete this and add the numbers later at home). Be sure to emphasize that it's strictly for their own personal use. Students who have already professed their faith may use the questionnaire as a reminder of what they professed.

For a closing prayer, ask the group to turn to Psalm 139 in their Bibles. Form two groups and take turns reading verses 1-14 responsively. End the prayer with everyone saying verses 23-24 in unison:

Search me, O God, and know my heart;
test me and know my anxious thoughts.
See if there is any offensive way in me,
and lead me in the way everlasting.

Another approach is to have students use the responsive readings on page 5 of their student book.

Session Extensions

1. Bag It!

For a fun approach to today's topics, prepare four "mystery" bags containing various props that relate to baptism, instruction, profession of faith, and the Lord's Supper. Working in groups of two or three, the students must discover what the contents of their bag suggest about a way that the church helps our faith grow. Here's a sample of what to put in the bags (be sure to add your own creative ideas):

- *baptism:* bar of soap, small bottle of water, diaper pin or baby rattle or baby blanket, drawing or photos of road signs (as symbol of a sacrament that is a sign of something else), birth certificate, Christ candle
- *instruction:* Bible, catechism book, marker or chalk, pen/pencil, paper, church school paper, notebook
- *profession of faith:* drawing or photo of road signs; picture of someone walking down a road (faith journey), church directory or other list of members of an organization, sketch (stick figures) of kids in front of church, microphone, voting ballot for elders/deacons, heart-shaped piece of paper
- *communion:* slice of bread, grapes, cross, picture of human body, picture of vial of blood, picture of people communicating with each other, small drinking glass

The groups should report what they guessed and why. Use this activity as an introduction to the session and to today's topic.

2. T-shirts and Other Gifts

You may want to provide a special gift to remind each student of the time you spent together and what you learned. One idea is to provide T-shirts with your church's name and symbol or logo on it; or "I Discovered My Church!"; or "My Church Includes Me!" You can make inexpensive T-shirt transfers using most inkjet printers and special iron-on transfers that you can purchase at office-supply stores. Your students can bring in their own T-shirts and you can iron them on as part of your activities during this last session. The kids could take turns signing their names on each other's shirts. Or you could distribute small pins, certificates, cards, or relevant books.

Extra Session

It's crucial for teens to recognize the idea that we are on a *lifelong* faith journey. No doubt this has come out in the session you've just taught. But if you have the time and the inclination, you can schedule an extra session to bring out the idea even more strongly. What follows is a brief outline for such a session.

Opening

Describe a recent trip you enjoyed, maybe passing around some photos as you talk. Have kids talk about their favorite trip or vacation. Bridge to the idea that we are all on a faith journey, a walk with Jesus along the road of our lives, a trip that begins at birth and ends with our going to a new place to be forever with our Lord.

Bible Study

Peter's faith journey is full of lessons for our own walk with God. Distribute Bibles and station five readers in a row to represent a kind of time line of key events in Peter's life. Give a notecard to each reader with the location of one of the following passages written on it (number each card as shown):
1. Mark 1:16-18
2. Matthew 16:13-18
3. John 13:33-38
4. John 18:15-18, 25-27
5. John 21:15-22

Ask for a volunteer to pantomime the emotions and reactions of Peter as each passage is read. Drape a "Peter" namecard around his or her neck. If you've got enough students, trade off the role of Peter for each passage that's read (the person reading the passage can pick someone to act out the passage). Then go through the passages in the sequence above, making a kind of "living timeline" of Peter's life as the passages are read and pantomimed.

Afterward, lead the group in a discussion of what we can learn about our own faith journeys from Peter's (they can do this in small groups, if you wish). Here are a few possibilities to consider:

- Our faith journeys have their high points and low points. High points for Peter are his being called by Jesus, his strong "profession of faith," his being called the rock on which Jesus would build the church, his being reinstated by Jesus. Low points include his bragging that he will follow Jesus to the death, Jesus' prediction of his denial, the denial itself, and his being asked repeatedly by Jesus if he loved Jesus.
- While we often fail Jesus, he never fails us.
- Jesus can use us to help build his church even through we aren't "super Christians." Note how Jesus calls Peter to "feed my sheep" even after he discovers Peter's weaknesses. Peter went on to become a powerful and persuasive leader of the early Christian church.
- Following Jesus is a lifelong task. Notice how Jesus' first and (nearly) last words to Peter were "Follow me." We need to renew our commitment to follow Jesus at many points in our lives. And we will always be learning what it means to follow Jesus.

Application

Have students make their own time lines of their spiritual journeys. Hand out a sheet of newsprint and markers to each student. Have them draw a line representing their life thus far (label that section "the past") and continue the line into a section labeled "the future." The general idea is to write in some approximate dates and events, some of a spiritual nature, some more general, some in the "past" section, some in the "future" section as possibilities.

Here are some examples of dates to include: date of birth; baptism; started church school; started school; Grandma died; began reading Bible before bed; attended VBS; started going to youth group; went on cool vacation; did service project with youth group; Dad lost job, prayed a lot; first part-time job; went to Christian summer camp, made commitment to Jesus; made or will make profession of faith; took or will take first communion; start high school; get my own car; graduate from high school; first real job; start college; have family of my own.

Be sensitive to students who are new Christians, making sure you don't assume that every child was born and raised in the church. Make this a relaxing, fun activity by providing some snacks and upbeat background music and letting the kids have a good time while they work.

Closing

In small groups, invite kids to share one spiritual "milestone" from the "past" section of their time lines and one way they would like to grow as Christians. Close by having the people in the small groups pray for each other. Pray that God would help them to serve him right now and to grow as Christians in the future.